BLOOM
Founded by | arihant

Olympiad ACE

A Comprehensive Practice Book

for School Olympiads & Talent Search Exams

GENERAL KNOWLEDGE

Class 9

by

Suman Bharti

Olympiad ACE

BLOOM

Bloom Cap Edu Ventures Pvt. Ltd.

卐 **Administrative & Production Office**

'Ramchhaya' 4577/15, Agarwal Road, Darya Ganj, New Delhi -110002
Tele: 011- 47630600, 43518550

卐 **PRICE:** ₹125.00

Published by Arihant Publications (I) Ltd.

For further information about the books log on to
www.bloomcap.org

Follow us on

Preface

"Future belongs to those Who prepares for it today"

School Olympiads are National & International level competitions conducted by different Government, Non-Government & Educational Organisations with the purpose of making the children ready to face competitive exams. The challenging Questions asked in Olympiads motivate them to learn more & more and bring out the best result with improved academic performance. The Awards & Scholarship offered by Olympiads motivate children to aspire & strive for doing better and emerge out to be the best.

GK Olympiads

GK is the knowledge of every aspect of the human life, which may or may not be the part of routine academic studies but very important for the overall personality development of the students. It is more or less connected with the attentiveness and awareness. There can be different domains of GK like; History, Geography, Polity, Culture, Discovery, Sports, Current Affairs etc.

GK Olympiads help students in understanding the importance of General Knowledge and updations about National & International Affairs in daily life.

'Bloom GK Olympiad Study Book Class 9' is a perfect resource to Study & Practice for Olympiad Exams and other National & State Level Talent Search Exams & Other Competitions.

Some Special Features of Bloom GK Olympiad Study Books are;

- Complete coverage of all the topics related to GK;. History, Geography, Environment, Polity, Science, Sports, etc.
- Chapterwise Exercises having different types of Objective Questions.
- Olympiad Pattern Practice Sets at the end.

This book is prepared by Expert Panel with the utmost care, still if you have any suggestions regarding its improvement then feel free to contact us at support@bloomcap.org. We will try to inculcate your suggestions in the further editions.

Contents

Chapter 01

Ancient History

MCQs 1 Mark Questions

1. Which among the following was the main occupation of Paleolithic (Old stone) people?
(a) Agriculture
(b) Fishing
(c) Hunting
(d) None of the above

2. The Indus Valley Civilisation belongs to the............ .
(a) Mesolithic period
(b) Chalcolithic period
(c) Neolithic period
(d) Paleolithic period

3. Name the site of Indus Valley Civilisation which is presently located in Pakistan.
(a) Kalibangan
(b) Harappa
(c) Alamgirpur
(d) Lothal

4. The main occupation of the people of the Indus Valley Civilisation was ....
(a) agriculture
(b) fishing
(c) warfare
(d) hunting

5. In which of the following sites of Indus Valley Civilisation, a clay model of plough has been found?
(a) Rakhigarhi
(b) Banawali
(c) Kalibangan
(d) Mitathal

6. Which among the following is the largest civilisation in the world?
(a) China Civilisation
(b) Indus Valley Civilisation
(c) Mesopotamian Civilisation
(d) Egypt Civilisation

7. Kalibangan, from the Indus Valley Civilisation is famous for which of the following?
(a) Pottery
(b) Sea Port
(c) Rock Cut Architecture
(d) Cotton Cultivation

8. Which is/are the most famous seal found from the Harrapan Civilisation?
(a) Animal seal
(b) Pashupati seal
(c) Unicorn seal
(d) All of the above

9. Which one of the following Indus Valley Civilisation sites gives evidence of a stadium?
(a) Harappa
(b) Kalibangan
(c) Dholavira
(d) Mohenjodaro

10. Identify the type of seal which was the most popular in Harappan culture.
(a) Oval
(b) Cylindrical
(c) Rounded
(d) Quadrate

11. The words Satyameva Jayate in the State Emblem adopted by the Government of India have been taken from .... Upanishad.
(a) Aitareya
(b) Mundaka
(c) Adhyatma
(d) Prasna

12. Which among the following is the Upaveda of Rigveda?
(a) Ayurveda
(b) Shilpaveda
(c) Gandhraveda
(d) Dhanuraveda

13. Complete the given analogy.
Panini : Ashtadhyayi :: ? : Malavikagnimitram
(a) Amoghavarsha
(b) Ravikirti
(c) Kalidasa
(d) Bilhana

14. Buddhist religious scripture 'Tripitaka' was written in........... .
(a) Prakrit
(b) Pali
(c) Sanskrit
(d) Hindi

15. Which among the following mudras is the gesture of Buddha as depicted in his first sermon?
(a) Abhaya Mudra
(b) Dhyana Mudra
(c) Dharmachakra Mudra
(d) Bhumisparsha Mudra

16. Chandragupta Maurya was succeeded by............. .
(a) Ashoka
(b) Harsha
(c) Bindusara
(d) Ajatashatru

17. .... is known as 'the Napoleon of Ancient India'.
(a) Pushyamitra Sunga
(b) Samudragupta
(c) Kanishka
(d) Chandragupta Maurya

18. Who among the following was the ruler during Alexander's invasion of India?
(a) Dhana Nanda
(b) Udayin
(c) Mahapadma Nanda
(d) Harshavardhana

19. Complete the given analogy.
Chandragupta II : Fa-Hien : : ? : Hiuen Tsang
(a) Ashoka
(b) Harsha
(c) Kanishka
(d) Vasudeva

20. Who among the following composed Prayag-Prashasti inscription during the Gupta period?
(a) Harisena
(b) Veerasena
(c) Banabhatta
(d) Asvaghosa

21. Which among the following is considered to be the official law book of the Guptas?
(a) Manusmriti
(b) Parashara Smriti
(c) Yajnavalkya Smriti
(d) Vyasa Smriti

22. Who among the following Gupta kings was first to issue silver coins?
(a) Chandragupta I
(b) Samudragupta
(c) Chandragupta II
(d) Kumaragupta

23. Who was the foremost astronomer and mathematician of the Gupta period?
(a) Aryabhatta
(b) Varahamihira
(c) Brahmagupta
(d) Banabhatta

24. Name the greatest scholar of Medical Science during ancient India.
(a) Charaka
(b) Vagbhatta
(c) Bhaskara
(d) Sushruta

25. Identify the most ancient learning center of India as shown in the picture given below.

(a) Nalanda
(b) Takshashila
(c) Odantapuri
(d) Vallabhi

26. Which of the following ancient Tamil Kingdoms came to be known from Sangam Literature?
(a) Chola
(b) Chera
(c) Pandya
(d) All of the above

27. Identify the incorrectly matched pair.

Ruler		Title
(a) Chandragupta	–	Sandrocottus
(b) Bindusara	–	Amitraghata
(c) Ashoka	–	Priyadarshi
(d) Chanakya	–	Samudragupta

28. Who was the author of the 'Harshacharita'?
(a) Banabhatta
(b) Kalidasa
(c) Harisena
(d) Chanakya

MCQs 2 Marks Questions

29. Which of the following statements is/are correct about Lord Buddha?
I. He was born in Kapilavastu.
II. He attained enlightenment at Bodh Gaya.
III. He discarded the vedas and vedic rituals.

Codes
(a) Only I
(b) Both I and II
(c) Both II and III
(d) All of the above

30. Read the given statements and select the option that correctly identifies true (T) and false (F) ones.

I. Copper is the first metal discovered by humans.

II. Lothal was a major port of the Indus Valley Civilisation.

III. Kalibangan is a Harappan site located in Rajasthan.

Codes

	I	II	III
(a)	F	T	F
(b)	F	F	T
(c)	T	T	T
(d)	T	F	F

31. There are two statements marked as Assertion (A) and Reason (R). Mark your answer as per the codes given below.

Assertion (A) The Hathigumpha inscriptions is the source of information about Kalinga ruler Kharavela.

Reason (R) Kalinga's King Kharavela was associated with Satavahana dynasty.

Codes

(a) Both A and R are true and R is the correct explanation of A

(b) Both A and R are true, but R is not the correct explanation of A

(c) A is true, but R is false

(d) A is false, but R is true

32. Match the following.

List I (Poet)	List II (Rulers)
A. Banabhatta	1. A famous poet in the court of Harshavardhana
B. Kalidasa	2. The court poet of Samudragupta
C. Harisena	3. A famous poet in the court of Chandragupta II

Codes

	A	B	C
(a)	1	3	2
(b)	3	1	2
(c)	1	2	3
(d)	2	3	1

33. Identify the rock cave shelter situated in India with the help of the information given below.

- It is considered to be one of the finest examples of ancient rock-cut caves, located near Aurangabad in Maharashtra.
- It is designated as UNESCO World Heritage Sites.

(a) Ajanta caves

(b) Ellora caves

(c) Both (a) and (b)

(d) Bhimbetka rock caves

Darken your choice with HB Pencil

1.	ⓐ ⓑ ⓒ ⓓ	7.	ⓐ ⓑ ⓒ ⓓ	13.	ⓐ ⓑ ⓒ ⓓ	19.	ⓐ ⓑ ⓒ ⓓ	25.	ⓐ ⓑ ⓒ ⓓ	31.	ⓐ ⓑ ⓒ ⓓ
2.	ⓐ ⓑ ⓒ ⓓ	8.	ⓐ ⓑ ⓒ ⓓ	14.	ⓐ ⓑ ⓒ ⓓ	20.	ⓐ ⓑ ⓒ ⓓ	26.	ⓐ ⓑ ⓒ ⓓ	32.	ⓐ ⓑ ⓒ ⓓ
3.	ⓐ ⓑ ⓒ ⓓ	9.	ⓐ ⓑ ⓒ ⓓ	15.	ⓐ ⓑ ⓒ ⓓ	21.	ⓐ ⓑ ⓒ ⓓ	27.	ⓐ ⓑ ⓒ ⓓ	33.	ⓐ ⓑ ⓒ ⓓ
4.	ⓐ ⓑ ⓒ ⓓ	10.	ⓐ ⓑ ⓒ ⓓ	16.	ⓐ ⓑ ⓒ ⓓ	22.	ⓐ ⓑ ⓒ ⓓ	28.	ⓐ ⓑ ⓒ ⓓ		
5.	ⓐ ⓑ ⓒ ⓓ	11.	ⓐ ⓑ ⓒ ⓓ	17.	ⓐ ⓑ ⓒ ⓓ	23.	ⓐ ⓑ ⓒ ⓓ	29.	ⓐ ⓑ ⓒ ⓓ		
6.	ⓐ ⓑ ⓒ ⓓ	12.	ⓐ ⓑ ⓒ ⓓ	18.	ⓐ ⓑ ⓒ ⓓ	24.	ⓐ ⓑ ⓒ ⓓ	30.	ⓐ ⓑ ⓒ ⓓ		

Chapter 02

Medieval History

MCQs 1 Mark Questions

1. Gita Govinda is one of the famous Indian poem written in Sanskrit language by ....
   (a) Jayachandra (b) Jayasimha
   (c) Jayadeva (d) Jayant

2. Who was the founder of Slave Dynasty?
   (a) Balban
   (b) Razia Sultan
   (c) Qutb-ud-Din Aibak
   (d) Iltutmish

3. ...... was the first and only female ruler of medieval India's Sultanate period.
   (a) Tara Bai
   (b) Razia Sultan
   (c) Gulbadan Begum
   (d) Nur Jahan

4. Who among the following established Delhi as the capital of Sultanate?
   (a) Muizzuddin Muhammad Ghori
   (b) Qutb-ud-Din Aibak
   (c) Razia Sultan
   (d) Iltutmish

5. Qutb-ud-Din Aibak constructed Adhai din ka-Jhonpra mosque in ....
   (a) Delhi
   (b) Agra
   (c) Ajmer
   (d) Gwalior

6. Minhaj-us-Siraj was a court poet of which sultan of Delhi?
   (a) Qutb-ud-Din Aibak
   (b) Iltutmish
   (c) Nasiruddin Mahmud
   (d) Razia Sultan

7. Which dynasty of Delhi Sultanate ruled for the shortest period?
   (a) Khalji
   (b) Tughlaq
   (c) Sayyid
   (d) Lodi

8. Who was the first Sultan of Delhi to impose grazing tax or house tax?
   (a) Balban
   (b) Alauddin Khalji
   (c) Muhammad bin Tughluq
   (d) Firoz Shah Tughlaq

9. Which among the following Tughlaq Sultans founded the city of Tughlaqabad?
(a) Muhammad bin Tughluq
(b) Ghiyas-ud-din Tughlaq
(c) Firoz Shah Tughlaq
(d) Ghiyas-ud-din Tughlaq Shah II

10. Identify the dynasty of Delhi Sultanate which claimed to be the descendant of the Prophet Muhammad.
(a) Khalji Dynasty
(b) Lodi Dynasty
(c) Sayyid Dynasty
(d) Tughlaq Dynasty

11. Who among the following Sultans of Delhi founded the city of Agra?
(a) Alauddin Khalji
(b) Balban
(c) Sikandar Lodi
(d) Muhammad bin Tughluq

12. Which of the following languages was patronised by the Delhi Sultans?
(a) Arabic
(b) Turkey
(c) Persian
(d) Urdu

13. Humayun Nama, the biography of Humayun was written by .... in Persian language.
(a) Shaista Khan
(b) Razia Sultan
(c) Gulbadan Begum
(d) Nur Jahan

14. Complete the given analogy.
1st Battle of Panipat : 1526 :: Battle of Khanwa : ?
(a) 1527
(b) 1528
(c) 1529
(d) 1530

15. Identify the ruler who constructed Ibadat Khana at Fatehpur Sikri.
(a) Akbar (b) Jahangir
(c) Shah Jahan (d) Aurangzeb

16. Which of the following monuments has one of the largest dome in the world?
(a) Sher Shah's Tomb, Sasaram
(b) Jama Masjid, Delhi
(c) Tomb of Ghiyasuddin Tughlaq, Delhi
(d) Gol Gumbaz, Bijapur

17. ....translated the Bhagavad Gita and Upanishads into the Persian language.
(a) Jahangir (b) Abu'l Fazl
(c) Dara Shikoh (d) Aurangzeb

18. Which one of the following monuments of Delhi Sultanate is included in the list of a World Heritage Site?
(a) Qutub Minar
(b) Alia Darwaza
(c) Quwat-Ul-Islam Mosque
(d) Lodi Garden

19. Complete the given analogy.
Brihadeshwara Temple : Rajaraja I :: Gangaikonda Cholapuram : ?
(a) Rajendra I (b) Aditya Chola
(c) Parantaka I (d) Rajaraja I

20. Identify the monument of India as shown in the picture given below.

(a) Tomb of Iltutmish (b) Tughlaqabad Fort
(c) Jama Masjid (d) Safdarjung Tomb

21. The institutions of Jagir and Mansab system were introduced by the............ .
(a) Mongols (b) Persians
(c) Mughals (d) Tughlaqs

22. Who established the Vijayanagara Empire?
(a) Krishnadeva Raya
(b) Harihar and Bukka
(c) Vir Pandya
(d) Narsingh Dev

MCQs 2 Marks Questions

23. Consider the following statements and select the correct option.
I. Qutb-ud-Din Aibak was a Turkish slave of Muhammad Ghori, who played an important part in the expansion of the Turkish Sultanate in India.
II. Qutb-ud-Din Aibak was known as 'Lakh Baksh' for his generosity.
III. Qutb-ud-Din Aibak was the first Muslim Sultanate ruler in Northern India.

Codes
(a) Only I (b) Only II
(c) I, II and III (d) Only III

24. Read the given statements and select the option that correctly identifies true (T) and false (F) ones.
I. The foundation for the Mughal painting was laid by Humayun while staying in Persia.
II. Red Fort of Delhi was constructed during the reign of Akbar.
III. 'Tansen' was the title given to Ram Tanu Pandey by the Mughal Emperor Akbar.
IV. Babur was the founder of the Mughal Empire which was established in 1526.

Codes

	I	II	III	IV
(a)	T	T	T	T
(b)	F	T	F	F
(c)	T	F	T	T
(d)	F	F	T	F

25. Consider the following statements associated with Akbar and choose the correct option.
I. Akbar patronised Tansen of Gwalior.
II. During Akbar's reign, the Humayun's tomb was built.
III. Persian language became widespread in the reign of Mughal Emperor Akbar.

Codes
(a) Only I
(b) Both I and II
(c) Both I and III
(d) All of the above

26. Read the given statements and select the option that correctly identifies true (T) and false (F) ones.
I. Zabti system was introduced by Akbar.
II. Akbar introduced the Mansabdari system.
III. Jharoka Darshan was introduced by Akbar.
IV. Aurangzeb was also called Zinda Pir.

Codes

	I	II	III	IV
(a)	T	T	T	F
(b)	F	T	F	F
(c)	T	T	T	T
(d)	F	F	T	F

27. Identify the famous personality with the help of the information given below.

- He was a poet, historian and musician associated with the Royal courts of more than seven rulers of Delhi Sultanate.
- He is popularly known as the Father of Hindi Khari Boli or 'Parrot of India'.

(a) Amir Khusrau
(b) Al-Biruni
(c) Minhaj-us-Siraj
(d) Ziauddin Barani

28. There are two statements marked as Assertion (A) and Reason (R). Mark your answer as per the codes given below.

Assertion (A) Babur won the first Battle of Panipat.

Reason (R) Babur was the first to introduce the use of Cannons in India.

Codes

(a) Both A and R are true and R is the correct explanation of A
(b) Both A and R are true, but R is not the correct explanation of A
(c) A is true, but R is false
(d) A is false, but R is true

Darken your choice with HB Pencil

1.	ⓐ ⓑ ⓒ ⓓ	6.	ⓐ ⓑ ⓒ ⓓ	11.	ⓐ ⓑ ⓒ ⓓ	16.	ⓐ ⓑ ⓒ ⓓ	21.	ⓐ ⓑ ⓒ ⓓ	26.	ⓐ ⓑ ⓒ ⓓ
2.	ⓐ ⓑ ⓒ ⓓ	7.	ⓐ ⓑ ⓒ ⓓ	12.	ⓐ ⓑ ⓒ ⓓ	17.	ⓐ ⓑ ⓒ ⓓ	22.	ⓐ ⓑ ⓒ ⓓ	27.	ⓐ ⓑ ⓒ ⓓ
3.	ⓐ ⓑ ⓒ ⓓ	8.	ⓐ ⓑ ⓒ ⓓ	13.	ⓐ ⓑ ⓒ ⓓ	18.	ⓐ ⓑ ⓒ ⓓ	23.	ⓐ ⓑ ⓒ ⓓ	28.	ⓐ ⓑ ⓒ ⓓ
4.	ⓐ ⓑ ⓒ ⓓ	9.	ⓐ ⓑ ⓒ ⓓ	14.	ⓐ ⓑ ⓒ ⓓ	19.	ⓐ ⓑ ⓒ ⓓ	24.	ⓐ ⓑ ⓒ ⓓ		
5.	ⓐ ⓑ ⓒ ⓓ	10.	ⓐ ⓑ ⓒ ⓓ	15.	ⓐ ⓑ ⓒ ⓓ	20.	ⓐ ⓑ ⓒ ⓓ	25.	ⓐ ⓑ ⓒ ⓓ		

Chapter 03

Modern History and National Movement

MCQs 1 Mark Questions

1. .... were the first European who came to India for trade.
(a) The English (b) The French
(c) The Portuguese (d) The Dutch

2. Who was the Nawab of Bengal at the time of the Battle of Plassey?
(a) Alivardi Khan
(b) Murshid Quli Khan
(c) Shuja-ud-Daula
(d) Siraj-ud-Daulah

3. .... was the first major victory of East India Company won in India.
(a) Battle of Seringapatam
(b) Battle of Plassey
(c) Battle of Buxar
(d) Battle of Panipat

4. Which of the following Governor-Generals of India introduced the Permanent Settlement?
(a) Thomas Munro
(b) Holt Mackenzie
(c) Lord Cornwallis
(d) Robert Clive

5. Which of the following Governor-Generals introduced the services of railway and telegraph system?
(a) Lord Cornwallis
(b) Lord Bentinck
(c) Lord Dalhousie
(d) Lord Wellesley

6. Identify the incorrectly matched pair.

	Governal- General/ Viceroy		Position
(a)	Warren Hastings	–	1st Governor-General of Bengal
(b)	William Bentinck	–	1st Governor-General of India
(c)	Lord Canning	–	1st Viceroy of India
(d)	Lord Mountbatten	–	Last Governor-General of Bengal

7. Complete the given analogy.
Ruler of Mysore : Tipu Sultan :: ? : Ranjit Singh
(a) Maharaja of Gwalior
(b) Maharaja of Sikh Empire
(c) Last Mughal Emperor
(d) Nawab of Bengal

8. Which one of the following slogans was given by Swami Dayananda Saraswati?
(a) Go Back to the Vedas
(b) Do or Die
(c) Aaram Haram Hai
(d) Vande Mataram

9. Who among the following was the founder of Satya Shodhak Samaj?
(a) Jyotiba Phule
(b) Sarojini Naidu
(c) Pandita Ramabai
(d) Sri Narayana Guru

10. The first movement launched against the British in India was ....
(a) Swadeshi Movement
(b) Khilafat Movement
(c) Quit India Movement
(d) Non-Cooperation Movement

11. Who among the following was the founder of Prathana Samaj?
(a) Atmaram Panduranga
(b) Dayananda Saraswati
(c) Raja Ram Mohan Roy
(d) Swami Vivekananda

12. Which among the following given personality, is popularly known as the 'Father of Indian Unrest'?
(a) Bal Gangadhar Tilak
(b) Dadabhai Naoroji
(c) Gopal Krishna Gokhale
(d) Mahatma Gandhi

13. The first session of the Indian National Congress was held in December 1885 in ....
(a) Calcutta
(b) Bombay
(c) Delhi
(d) Madras

14. Who amongst the following is considered to be the Father of 'Local Self-Government' in India?
(a) Lord Dalhousie (b) Lord Canning
(c) Lord Curzon (d) Lord Ripon

15. In which session, the Indian National Congress split into two parts that are Moderates and Extremists?
(a) Surat Session
(b) Nagpur Session
(c) Bombay Session
(d) Allahabad Session

16. Who among the following was the political Guru of Mahatma Gandhi?
(a) Gopal Krishna Gokhale
(b) Dayananda Saraswati
(c) Rabindranath Tagore
(d) None of the above

17. Identify the incorrectly matched pair.

National Movement	Year
(a) Jallianwala Bagh Massacre	– 1919
(b) Civil Disobedience Movement	– 1924
(c) Dandi March	– 1930
(d) Quit India Movement	– 1942

18. Who among the following started Non-Cooperation Movement during British India?
(a) Mahatma Gandhi
(b) Dadabhai Naoroji
(c) Gopal Krishna Gokhale
(d) Bal Gangadhar Tilak

19. ...... was the first Muslim President of the Indian National Congress and also served as the third President of Indian National Congress.
(a) Maulana Abul Kalam Azad
(b) Badruddin Tyabji
(c) Hakim Ajmal Khan
(d) Rahimtullah M Sayani

MCQs 2 Marks Questions

20. Match the following.

List I (Nickname)	List II (Freedom fighter)
A. Iron Man of India	1. Vallabhbhai Patel
B. Punjab Kesari	2. Lala Lajpat Rai
C. Loknayak	3. Jayaprakash Narayan
D. Deshbandhu	4. Chitranjan Das

Codes

	A	B	C	D		A	B	C	D
(a)	1	2	3	4	(b)	4	2	3	1
(c)	2	1	4	3	(d)	3	4	1	2

21. Identify the freedom fighter of India with the help of the information given below.

- He was an Indian author, freedom fighter and politician and popularly known as 'Punjab Kesari'.
- He was one of the founding member of Punjab National Bank and established the Dayanand Anglo-vedic school in Lahore in 1885.

(a) Lala Lajpat Rai (b) Bhagat Singh
(c) Ajit Singh (d) Gopal Krishna Gokhale

22. Read the following statements and select the correct option.

I. Veer Savarkar was a leading figure in the Hindu Mahasabha.

II. The Ramakrishna Mission was founded by Swami Vivekananda in 1897.

III. Brahmo Samaj was a social reform society founded by Jyotiba Phule in Pune, Maharashtra.

Codes

(a) Only I
(b) Only II
(c) Both I and II
(d) All of the above

23. Consider the following statements and choose the correct option.

I. The first English factory was set up on the banks of the river Hugli in 1651.

II. Lord Cornwallis became the first Governor-General of India in 1773.

III. On August 1733, the Mughal Emperor appointed the East India Company as the Diwan of Bengal.

Codes

(a) I and II (b) Only I
(c) II and III (d) Only III

24. There are two statements marked as Assertion (A) and Reason (R). Mark your answer as per the codes given below.

Assertion (A) Warren Hastings played a significant role in the expansion of company power.

Reason (R) Governor-General was the supreme head of the British administration.

Codes

(a) Both A and R are true and R is the correct explanation of A
(b) Both A and R are true, but R is not the correct explanation of A
(c) A is true, but R is false
(d) A is false, but R is true

Darken your choice with HB Pencil

1.	a	b	c	d	5.	a	b	c	d	9.	a	b	c	d	13.	a	b	c	d	17.	a	b	c	d	21.	a	b	c	d
2.	a	b	c	d	6.	a	b	c	d	10.	a	b	c	d	14.	a	b	c	d	18.	a	b	c	d	22.	a	b	c	d
3.	a	b	c	d	7.	a	b	c	d	11.	a	b	c	d	15.	a	b	c	d	19.	a	b	c	d	23.	a	b	c	d
4.	a	b	c	d	8.	a	b	c	d	12.	a	b	c	d	16.	a	b	c	d	20.	a	b	c	d	24.	a	b	c	d

Chapter 04

History of the World

MCQs 1 Mark Questions

1. Which among the following is the oldest civilisation in the world?
(a) Mesopotamian Civilisation
(b) Egyptian Civilisation
(c) Indus Valley Civilisation
(d) Chinese Civilisation

2. The world famous painting 'Mona Lisa' was painted by.................. .
(a) Vincent van Gogh
(b) Filippo Brunelleschi
(c) Michelangelo
(d) Leonardo da Vinci

3. Which among the following is related to the Glorious Revolution?
(a) USA (b) England
(c) China (d) Russia

4. Boston Tea Party protest was associated with the revolution of ....
(a) America (b) Italy
(c) French (d) India

5. Who among the following was the first President of the independent United States of America?
(a) George Washington
(b) Thomas Jefferson
(c) John Adams
(d) None of the above

6. Which of the following areas was under French colonial control?
(a) Vietnam
(b) Ceylon
(c) Malay Peninsula
(d) Indonesia

7. Which one of the following played an important role in the Unification of Italy?
(a) Joseph Mazzini
(b) Conte di Cavour
(c) Julius Caesar
(d) None of the above

8. Who among the following is associated with the 'Blood and Iron Policy'?
(a) Hitler
(b) Bismarck
(c) Karl Marx
(d) William I

9. The Great Depression was known as a period of ....
(a) political crisis (b) social crisis
(c) global crisis (d) economic crisis

10. The slogan Liberty, Equality, Fraternity was given during which of the following revolutions?
(a) Russian Revolution
(b) French Revolution
(c) American War of Independence
(d) Industrial Revolution

11. Who among the following was the king of France at the time of the French Revolution?

(a) Louis IX (b) Louis XIV
(c) Louis XVI (d) Marie Antoinette

12. Identify the incorrectly matched pair.

	Thinker		Work
(a)	John Locke	–	Two Treaties of Government
(b)	Rousseau	–	Social Contract
(c)	Montesquieu	–	The Spirit of the Law
(d)	Voltaire	–	Das Kapital

13. Which religion was followed by most of the people of Russia?

(a) Catholics
(b) Protestants
(c) Russian Orthodox Christianity
(d) None of the above

14. Name the Russian revolutionary, who founded the Communist Party.

(a) Karl Marx (b) Stalin
(c) Lenin (d) Trotsky

15. The central powers during the First World War included the countries like Germany, Bulgaria and ....

(a) Austria (b) Britain
(c) Russia (d) France

16. What was the name of the atom bomb dropped by USA on Hiroshima in Japan during the Second World War?

(a) Little Fly (b) Little Devil
(c) Little Boy (d) Fat Man

17. What is the name of Republic that was established in Germany after First World War?

(a) Republic of German Federation
(b) Republic of German Confederation
(c) German Republic State
(d) The Weimer Republic

18. Who among the following led the Bolshevik group during the Russian Revolution?

(a) Lenin (b) Karl Marx
(c) Fredrich Engels (d) Trotsky

19. What was the movement demanding the Rights to Vote for women called?

(a) Russian Orthodox' Christianity Movement
(b) Suffragette Movement
(c) Social Democratic Party Movement
(d) Revolutionary Movement

20. During Second World War, who among the following was the Commander General of Italy?

(a) Benito Mussolini (b) Kuniaki Koiso
(c) Karl Dönitz (d) None of these

MCQs 2 Marks Questions

21. Which of the following countries fought in Second World War?

I. Italy II. France
III. USSR IV. Japan

Choose the correct option.

(a) I and II
(b) I,II and III
(c) I,III and IV
(d) All of the above

22. Consider the following statements.

I. The emperor of Russia was called 'Czar'.
II. 'Duma' was the Russian Parliament before the Bolshevik Revolution took place.
III. The term 'Soviet' means a council of workers.

Which of the above statements is/are correct?

(a) Only I (b) Both I and II
(c) Both I and III (d) All of these

23. There are two statements marked as Assertion (A) and Reason (R). Mark your answer as per the codes given below.

Assertion (A) The First World War was the first modern industrial war.

Reason (R) There were 9 million people died and 20 million injured with the use of industrial arms.

Codes

(a) Both A and R are true and R is the correct explanation of A
(b) Both A and R are true, but R is not the correct explanation of A
(c) A is true, but R is false
(d) A is false, but R is true

24. Match the following.

List I (Philosopher)	**List II** (Related to)
A. Stalin	1. Father of Communism
B. John Locke	2. Czar of Russia
C. Nicholas II	3. Father of Liberalism
D. Karl Marx	4. Collectivisation Programme

Codes

	A	B	C	D		A	B	C	D
(a)	4	3	2	1	(b)	2	3	4	1
(c)	1	3	2	4	(d)	2	4	1	3

25. Read the given statements and select the option that correctly identifies true (T) and false (F) ones.

I. First World War was one of the great watershed in geopolitical history of 20th century.
II. Second World War, was a devastating global conflict that began in 1939.
III. The Second World War came to an end in May, 1945.
IV. United States entered into Second World War due to Japanese attack on Pearl Harbour.

Codes

	I	II	III	IV		I	II	III	IV
(a)	T	T	T	T	(b)	F	T	F	F
(c)	T	F	T	T	(d)	F	F	T	F

26. On the given outline map of the world, identify the Allied powers of the First World War.

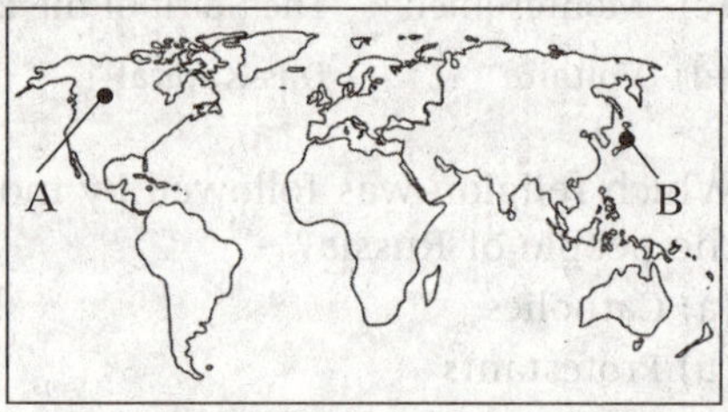

	A	B
(a)	France	Canada
(b)	Canada	Japan
(c)	Japan	United States
(d)	France	United States

27. Match the following.

List I	**List II**
A. 1914	1. First World War begins
B. 1917	2. The Petrograd Soviet meeting in the Duma
C. 1918	3. Proclamation of the Weimar Republic
D. 1919	4. Treaty of Versailles

Codes

	A	B	C	D		A	B	C	D
(a)	1	2	3	4	(b)	4	3	2	1
(c)	2	1	4	3	(d)	3	4	1	2

Darken your choice with HB Pencil

1. ⓐ ⓑ ⓒ ⓓ	6. ⓐ ⓑ ⓒ ⓓ	11. ⓐ ⓑ ⓒ ⓓ	16. ⓐ ⓑ ⓒ ⓓ	21. ⓐ ⓑ ⓒ ⓓ	26. ⓐ ⓑ ⓒ ⓓ
2. ⓐ ⓑ ⓒ ⓓ	7. ⓐ ⓑ ⓒ ⓓ	12. ⓐ ⓑ ⓒ ⓓ	17. ⓐ ⓑ ⓒ ⓓ	22. ⓐ ⓑ ⓒ ⓓ	27. ⓐ ⓑ ⓒ ⓓ
3. ⓐ ⓑ ⓒ ⓓ	8. ⓐ ⓑ ⓒ ⓓ	13. ⓐ ⓑ ⓒ ⓓ	18. ⓐ ⓑ ⓒ ⓓ	23. ⓐ ⓑ ⓒ ⓓ	
4. ⓐ ⓑ ⓒ ⓓ	9. ⓐ ⓑ ⓒ ⓓ	14. ⓐ ⓑ ⓒ ⓓ	19. ⓐ ⓑ ⓒ ⓓ	24. ⓐ ⓑ ⓒ ⓓ	
5. ⓐ ⓑ ⓒ ⓓ	10. ⓐ ⓑ ⓒ ⓓ	15. ⓐ ⓑ ⓒ ⓓ	20. ⓐ ⓑ ⓒ ⓓ	25. ⓐ ⓑ ⓒ ⓓ	

Chapter 05

Art and Culture

MCQs 1 Mark Questions

1. Tansen, a great musician was one of the Navaratnas in the court of ....
   (a) Jahangir
   (b) Shah Jahan
   (c) Akbar
   (d) Bahadur Shah

2. 'Khajuraho Dance Festival' is a famous event organised in which Indian state?
   (a) Gujarat
   (b) Bihar
   (c) Madhya Pradesh
   (d) Maharashtra

3. In which of the following festivals, boat races are a special feature?
   (a) Pongal
   (b) Navratri
   (c) Rongali Bihu
   (d) Onam

4. 'Thang Ta' a martial art form is associated with which state of India?
   (a) Mizoram
   (b) Nagaland
   (c) Manipur
   (d) Tripura

5. Which among the following temples of India is known as Black Pagoda?
   (a) Brihadeshwara Temple, Thanjavur
   (b) Sun Temple, Konark
   (c) Lord Jagannath Temple, Puri
   (d) Meenakshi Temple, Madurai

6. 'Hornbill Festival' is a cultural festival celebrated in which State?
   (a) Assam
   (b) Nagaland
   (c) West Bengal
   (d) Bihar

7. 'Jallikattu' is a bull-taming event, celebrated in which state?
   (a) Karnataka
   (b) Tamil Nadu
   (c) Andhra Pradesh
   (d) Odisha

8. Identify the incorrectly matched pair.

Renowned Personalities		Musical Instrument
(a) Bismillah Khan	–	Shehnai
(b) Amzad Ali Khan	–	Sarod
(c) Birju Maharaj	–	Kathak
(d) Zakir Hussain	–	Harmonium

9. Identify the state of India in which 'Madhubani', a style of folk paintings is popular.
(a) Uttar Pradesh
(b) Rajasthan
(c) Madhya Pradesh
(d) Bihar

10. Choose the correct statement regarding Indian dance forms.
(a) Ghoomar is a dance form of Punjab.
(b) Dumhal is a popular folk dance of Himachal Pradesh.
(c) Cholliya is the folk dance of Uttarakhand.
(d) Bihu is a classical dance of Odisha.

11. Who among the following was the painter of the famous painting called 'Bharat Mata'?
(a) Nandalal Bose
(b) Jamini Roy
(c) Gaganendranath Tagore
(d) Abanindranath Tagore

12. Complete the given analogy.
Punjab : Makki Di Roti :: ? : Dhokla
(a) Rajasthan
(b) Maharashtra
(c) Gujarat
(d) Tamil Nadu

13. English is the official language of which one of the following Indian states?
(a) Manipur
(b) Assam
(c) Tripura
(d) Nagaland

14. Dongri language is spoken in which of the following states/UT of India?
(a) Karnataka
(b) Jammu and Kashmir
(c) Assam
(d) Tripura

15. Name the language that is widely spoken by the people residing in Kerala.
(a) Malayalam
(b) Konkani
(c) Telugu
(d) Oriya

16. Identify the temple as depicted in the picture given below.

(a) Brihadeshwara Temple
(b) Lingaraj Temple
(c) Akshardham Temple
(d) Badrinath Temple

17. .... is the harvest festival that is celebrated in Assam that marks the beginning of the Assamese New Year.
(a) Bohag Bihu
(b) Lohri
(c) Makar Sankranti
(d) Onam

18. The famous 'Ganga Sagar Mela', an annual fair is held in which state of India?
(a) Bihar (b) Uttar Pradesh
(c) Jharkhand (d) West Bengal

19. The famous temple of India, Mahakaleshwar Temple is located at ....
(a) Port Blair, Andaman and Nicobar Islands
(b) Pune, Maharashtra
(c) Kohlapur, Maharashtra
(d) Ujjain, Madhya Pradesh

MCQs 2 Marks Questions

20. Which among the following are stringed instruments?

I. Sitar
II. Pakhawaj
III. Santoor
IV. Mridangam
V. Sarangi

Codes

(a) I, II and III
(b) I, III, IV and V
(c) II, III, IV and V
(d) I, III and V

21. Identify the name of the famous sculpture with the help of the information given below.

It is a famous bronze sculpture and a symbol of Indian culture. It belongs to the dynasty of 10th century. It is a sculpture of Lord Shiva.

(a) Mahakal
(b) Nataraja
(c) Shiv Murti
(d) Bhairava

22. Read the given statements and select the option that correctly identifies true (T) and false (F) ones.

I. The classical dance of Andhra Pradesh is Kuchipudi.
II. Phulkari painting is associated with the state of Punjab.
III. Sarhul festival is the most popular tribal celebration across the State of Jharkhand region.
IV. The famous folk dance of Rajasthan is Dandiya.

Codes

	I	II	III	IV		I	II	III	IV
(a)	F	T	T	F	(b)	F	F	F	T
(c)	T	T	T	F	(d)	T	F	F	T

23. There are two statements marked as Assertion (A) and Reason (R). Mark your answer as per the codes given below.

Assertion (A) Baisakhi is an important festival for the people of Sikh religion.

Reason (R) It marks the Sikh New Year and commemorates the formation of Khalsa Panth of warriors under Guru Gobind Singh in 1699.

Codes

(a) Both A and R are true and R is the correct explanation of A
(b) Both A and R are true, but R is not the correct explanation of A
(c) A is true, but R is false
(d) A is false, but R is true

24. Match the following.

List I (Heritage Sites of India)	List II (Location)
A. Humayun's Tomb	1. Uttar Pradesh
B. Sanchi Stupa	2. Bihar
C. Barabar Cave	3. Madhya Pradesh
D. Buland Darwaza	4. Delhi

Codes

	A	B	C	D
(a)	4	3	2	1
(b)	1	3	4	2
(c)	2	1	3	4
(d)	3	4	1	2

25. Consider the following statements regarding the Khajuraho temple and select the correct option.

I. It is a group of Hindu and Jain Temple in Madhya Pradesh.

II. These temples were built by Chandela Dynasty.

III. It is a UNESCO World Heritage sites.

Codes

(a) Only I

(b) I and II

(c) I and III

(d) All of the above

26. Identify the dance forms that are famous in the states marked as A and B on the map given below.

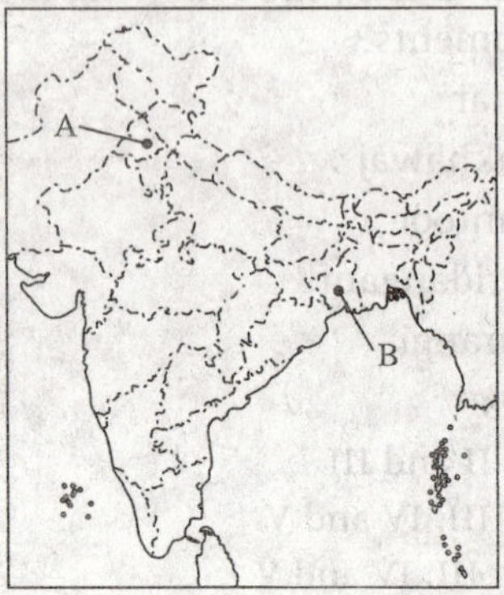

	A	B
(a)	Lavani	Sattriya
(b)	Giddha	Chhau
(c)	Kathak	Bharatanatyam
(d)	Garba	Odissi

Darken your choice with HB Pencil

1. ⓐ ⓑ ⓒ ⓓ	6. ⓐ ⓑ ⓒ ⓓ	11. ⓐ ⓑ ⓒ ⓓ	16. ⓐ ⓑ ⓒ ⓓ	21. ⓐ ⓑ ⓒ ⓓ	26. ⓐ ⓑ ⓒ ⓓ
2. ⓐ ⓑ ⓒ ⓓ	7. ⓐ ⓑ ⓒ ⓓ	12. ⓐ ⓑ ⓒ ⓓ	17. ⓐ ⓑ ⓒ ⓓ	22. ⓐ ⓑ ⓒ ⓓ	
3. ⓐ ⓑ ⓒ ⓓ	8. ⓐ ⓑ ⓒ ⓓ	13. ⓐ ⓑ ⓒ ⓓ	18. ⓐ ⓑ ⓒ ⓓ	23. ⓐ ⓑ ⓒ ⓓ	
4. ⓐ ⓑ ⓒ ⓓ	9. ⓐ ⓑ ⓒ ⓓ	14. ⓐ ⓑ ⓒ ⓓ	19. ⓐ ⓑ ⓒ ⓓ	24. ⓐ ⓑ ⓒ ⓓ	
5. ⓐ ⓑ ⓒ ⓓ	10. ⓐ ⓑ ⓒ ⓓ	15. ⓐ ⓑ ⓒ ⓓ	20. ⓐ ⓑ ⓒ ⓓ	25. ⓐ ⓑ ⓒ ⓓ	

Chapter 06

Universe

MCQs 1 Mark Questions

1. Which of the following planets is located nearest to the Sun?
   (a) Venus (b) Mercury
   (c) Saturn (d) Mars

2. Which planet rotates in the opposite direction than other planets in the Solar System?
   (a) Mars (b) Saturn
   (c) Uranus (d) Mercury

3. What cause the changes in seasons?
   (a) Earth's rotation and revolution
   (b) Earth's revolution
   (c) Earth's revolution and inclination of its axis
   (d) Earth's rotation and inclination of its axis

4. ………… are large objects made of dust and ice that revolve around the Sun in highly elliptical orbits.
   (a) Comets (b) Asteroids
   (c) Planets (d) Stars

5. The Big Bang Theory is related with which of the following phenomenon?
   (a) Continental Drift
   (b) Origin of the Himalayas
   (c) Eruption of Volcanoes
   (d) Origin of the Universe

6. Which of the following planets has largest number of natural satellites?
   (a) Jupiter (b) Mars
   (c) Saturn (d) Venus

7. The Sun is mainly composed of which of the following two elements?
   (a) Hydrogen and Nitrogen
   (b) Nitrogen and Helium
   (c) Hydrogen and Helium
   (d) All of the above

8. Which among the following constellation is used to locate the Polar star?
   (a) Ursa major (b) Orion
   (c) Centaurus (d) Cassiopeia

9. There are numerous tiny bodies which also move around the Sun. These bodies are called ………… .
   (a) asteroids (b) satellites
   (c) black holes (d) comets

10. Which of the following is known as innermost layer of the Earth?
    (a) Crust (b) Core (c) Mantle (d) Magma

11. Identify the incorrectly matched pair.
    (a) Mars – Red Planet
    (b) Jupiter – Largest Planet
    (c) Earth – Densest Planet
    (d) Venus – Coldest Planet

12. The equatorial plane and the orbital plane are inclined to each other at an angle of ………… .
    (a) 23.5° (b) 32.5°
    (c) 55.5° (d) 66.5°

13. The circle that divides the globe into day and night is called ....
(a) circle of darkness
(b) circle of day and night
(c) circle of illumination
(d) None of the above

14. Which is a celestial phenomenon occurring due to stars?
(a) Ozone Hole (b) Black Hole
(c) Both (a) and (b) (d) Comet

15. The Earth is at the largest distance from the Sun (Apehelion) on which date?
(a) 21st June (b) 3rd January
(c) 4th July (d) 23rd September

16. Who among the following first claimed that the Earth revolves spherically around the Sun?
(a) Isaac Newton (b) Kepler
(c) Copernicus (d) Ptolemy

17. An equinox occurs when the Sun is vertically above the ....
(a) Tropic of Capricorn (b) Tropic of Cancer
(c) Poles (d) Equator

18. How much time does a Sun ray take to reach the Earth?
(a) 8 minutes (b) 9 minutes
(c) 10 minutes (d) 12 minutes

19. Complete the given analogy.
Torrid Zone : Hot climate : : Temperate Zone : ?
(a) Moderate climate (b) Cold climate
(c) Very hot climate (d) Very cold climate

20. Which of the following planets is known as Earth's twin?
(a) Mars (b) Saturn (c) Venus (d) Uranus

21. Which one of the following planets takes the same number of days for rotation and revolution?
(a) Earth and Mars (b) Mercury and Venus
(c) Venus and Mars (d) Jupiter and Mars

22. Which of the following statements is incorrect about Uranus?
(a) It is known as the Green Planet and it has faint rings around it.
(b) It is an Ice Giant planet.
(c) It has 27 Moons.
(d) It rotates from West to East.

23. Name the first artificial satellite of the Earth.
(a) Sputnik-I (b) Explorer-I
(c) Aryabhatta (d) Luna-3

24. Which among the following celestial bodies bear, 'The Sea of Tranquility' and 'The Ocean of Storms'?
(a) Mars (b) Moon (c) Venus (d) Sun

25. What are the two basic types of planets in the Solar System?
(a) Ice and Gas
(b) Terrestrial and Jovian
(c) Tomaso and Jerrian
(d) None of the above

26. Which of these layers of the atmosphere consists of the ozone layer that is responsible for absorbing the Ultra-Violet (UV) light?
(a) Troposphere (b) Mesosphere
(c) Stratosphere (d) None of these

MCQs 2 Marks Questions

27. Select the chronology of the planets according to their size.
I. Mercury II. Mars
III. Venus IV. Earth

Codes
(a) I, III, IV, II (b) IV, I, II, III
(c) III, I, II, IV (d) II, I, III, IV

28. Match the following.

List I	List II
A. Longest Day	1. 23rd September
B. Winter Solstice	2. 22nd December
C. Spring Equinox	3. 21st June
D. Autumn Equinox	4. 21st March

Codes

	A	B	C	D		A	B	C	D
(a)	4	3	2	1	(b)	1	3	4	2
(c)	2	1	3	4	(d)	3	2	4	1

29. There are two statements marked as Assertion (A) and Reason (R). Mark your answer as per the codes given below.

Assertion (A) The Moon is a planetary mass object with a differentiated rocky body.

Reason (R) Moon is a satellite of the Earth and it does not emit light of its own.

Codes

(a) Both A and R are true and R is the correct explanation of A

(b) Both A and R are true, but R is not the correct explanation of A

(c) A is true, but R is false

(d) A is false, but R is true

30. Read the given statements and select the option that correctly identifies true (T) and false (F) ones.

I. The Earth travels around the Sun in an elliptical orbit.

II. The Equator receives direct rays of the Sun throughout the year.

III. The gravitational pull of the Sun affects the seasons.

Codes

	I	II	III		I	II	III
(a)	F	T	T	(b)	F	F	F
(c)	T	T	T	(d)	T	F	F

31. There are two statements marked as Assertion (A) and Reason (R). Mark your answer as per the codes given below.

Assertion (A) Planets are non-luminous bodies.

Reason (R) They reflect the light of the Sun.

Codes

(a) Both A and R are true and R is the correct explanation of A

(b) Both A and R are true, but R is not the correct explanation of A

(c) A is true, but R is false

(d) A is false, but R is true

32. Consider the following pairs.

I. Mercury – Jovian planet

II. Venus – Duration of day longer than that of year

III. Saturn – A planet having density less than that of water

Which of the pairs given above is/are correctly matched?

(a) Only I

(b) II and III

(c) I and III

(d) All of the above

Darken your choice with HB Pencil

1.	ⓐ ⓑ ⓒ ⓓ	7.	ⓐ ⓑ ⓒ ⓓ	13.	ⓐ ⓑ ⓒ ⓓ	19.	ⓐ ⓑ ⓒ ⓓ	25.	ⓐ ⓑ ⓒ ⓓ	31.	ⓐ ⓑ ⓒ ⓓ
2.	ⓐ ⓑ ⓒ ⓓ	8.	ⓐ ⓑ ⓒ ⓓ	14.	ⓐ ⓑ ⓒ ⓓ	20.	ⓐ ⓑ ⓒ ⓓ	26.	ⓐ ⓑ ⓒ ⓓ	32.	ⓐ ⓑ ⓒ ⓓ
3.	ⓐ ⓑ ⓒ ⓓ	9.	ⓐ ⓑ ⓒ ⓓ	15.	ⓐ ⓑ ⓒ ⓓ	21.	ⓐ ⓑ ⓒ ⓓ	27.	ⓐ ⓑ ⓒ ⓓ		
4.	ⓐ ⓑ ⓒ ⓓ	10.	ⓐ ⓑ ⓒ ⓓ	16.	ⓐ ⓑ ⓒ ⓓ	22.	ⓐ ⓑ ⓒ ⓓ	28.	ⓐ ⓑ ⓒ ⓓ		
5.	ⓐ ⓑ ⓒ ⓓ	11.	ⓐ ⓑ ⓒ ⓓ	17.	ⓐ ⓑ ⓒ ⓓ	23.	ⓐ ⓑ ⓒ ⓓ	29.	ⓐ ⓑ ⓒ ⓓ		
6.	ⓐ ⓑ ⓒ ⓓ	12.	ⓐ ⓑ ⓒ ⓓ	18.	ⓐ ⓑ ⓒ ⓓ	24.	ⓐ ⓑ ⓒ ⓓ	30.	ⓐ ⓑ ⓒ ⓓ		

Chapter 07

Physical Features of India

MCQs 1 Mark Questions

1. Name the Northern most range of the Himalayan mountains in India.
(a) Shivalik (b) Lesser Himalaya
(c) Himadri (d) Aravalli

2. Which one of the following pairs of states are the Easternmost and Westernmost states of India?
(a) Assam and Gujarat
(b) Assam and Rajasthan
(c) Arunachal Pradesh and Rajasthan
(d) Arunachal Pradesh and Gujarat

3. Name the country which shares land boundaries with India in the East.
(a) Bhutan (b) Bangladesh
(c) China (d) Vietnam

4. In which among the following hemispheres, India is located?
(a) Northern and Eastern
(b) Northern and Western
(c) Southern and Western
(d) Southern and Eastern

5. Name the country with which India shares Line of Actual Control.
(a) Nepal (b) Bhutan
(c) China (d) Pakistan

6. Which among the following physical features of India is made up of alluvial deposits?
(a) The Deccan Plateau
(b) Islands
(c) Northern Plain
(d) Coastal Plain

7. Identify the Himalayan passes which is situated between India and China.
(a) Shenkota (b) Thalghat
(c) Bhorghat (d) Shipki La

8. Name the strait which lies between India and Sri Lanka.
(a) Palk Strait (b) Malacca Strait
(c) Bering Strait (d) None of these

9. Which of the following physical features of India forms the Northern frontiers?
(a) Himalayan Mountain Range
(b) Karakoram Range
(c) Aravalli Range
(d) Satpura Range

10. The Indo-Gangetic Plain, which runs between ...., lies just South of the Himalayas.
(a) Indus and Ganges rivers
(b) Brahmaputra and Ganges rivers
(c) Godavari and Ganges rivers
(d) Indus and Brahmaputra rivers

11. Rihand Dam is located on river Rihand, a tributary of ....
(a) Sutlej river (b) Son river
(c) Godavari river (d) Brahmaputra river

12. In which division of the Himalayas are the famous valley of Kashmir, Kangra and Kullu located?
(a) Himachal (b) Himadri
(c) Shivalik (d) Duns

13. Complete the given analogy.
Uttarakhand : China :: ? : Bangladesh
(a) Odisha (b) Arunachal Pradesh
(c) Chhattisgarh (d) Meghalaya

14. Identify the correctly matched pair.

	Mountains/hills		States
(a)	Aravalli Range	–	Gujarat
(b)	Cardamom Hills	–	Odisha
(c)	Zaskar Range	–	Kashmir Region
(d)	Vindhya Range	–	Uttarakhand

15. Anamudi is the highest peak in the ....
(a) Himalayan Mountains
(b) Western Ghats
(c) Eastern Ghats
(d) Peninsular Plateau

16. Which among the following is agriculturally the most productive part of India?
(a) Peninsular Plateau
(b) Coastal Plains
(c) Northern Plains
(d) Himalayan Mountain

17. Identify the loftiest and one of the most rugged mountain barriers of the world.
(a) Aravalli Ranges
(b) Sulaiman Ranges
(c) Himalayan Mountains
(d) Kunlun Mountains

18. .... Hills of Tamil Nadu lie at the junction of the Eastern and Western Ghats.
(a) Anamudi (b) Nilgiri
(c) Mahendragiri (d) Aravalli

19. Which of the following physical division of India has the oldest landmass?
(a) The Himalayas
(b) The Northern Plain
(c) The Peninsular Plateau
(d) The Indian Desert

20. .... is the largest salt water lake on the Eastern Coast of Odisha and lies to the South of Mahanadi delta.
(a) Wular Lake (b) Chilika Lake
(c) Dal Lake (d) Loktak Lake

21. In which part of Himalayan is 'Karewa' landform found?
(a) North-East Himalaya
(b) Eastern Himalaya
(c) Himachal-Uttarakhand Himalaya
(d) Kashmir Himalaya

22. Which of the following plateaus is not a part of Central Highlands?
(a) Chota Nagpur Plateau
(b) Bundelkhand
(c) Baghelkhand
(d) Deccan Trap

23. .... is the longest river of peninsular India and the second longest river of India after Ganga.
(a) Krishna (b) Godavari
(c) Narmada (d) Brahmaputra

24. In which one of the following islands of India is an active volcano found?
(a) Barren Island
(b) Havelock Island
(c) Marshall Island
(d) Swaraj Island

25. The Pir Panjal Range is located in which of the following States or Union Territories?
(a) Arunachal Pradesh
(b) Jammu and Kashmir
(c) Punjab
(d) Uttarakhand

26. The extreme Southernmost point of India, i.e. Pygmalion point is located in which of the following islands?
(a) Arabian Sea Island
(b) Bay of Bengal Island
(c) Offshore Island
(d) None of the above

27. Identify the physical feature of India as depicted on the picture given below.

(a) Peninsula (b) Island
(c) Plateau (d) Mountain

28. What is/are the composition(s) of the Himalayan Mountain?
(a) Highly compressed rocks
(b) Highly altered rocks
(c) Both (a) and (b)
(d) None of the above

MCQs 2 Marks Questions

29. Arrange the following regions of the Northern plains in sequence from North to South direction.
I. Bhangar II. Khadar
III. Bhabhar IV. Terai

Codes
(a) I, II, III, IV (b) II, IV, III, I
(c) II, III, IV, I (d) III, IV, I, II

30. Match the following.

List I (Himalayas)	**List II** (Rivers)
A. Nepal Himalayas	1. Indus-Satluj
B. Assam Himalayas	2. Teesta- Dihang
C. Kumaon Himalayas	3. Kali -Teesta
D. Punjab Himalayas	4. Satluj - Kali

Codes

	A	B	C	D
(a)	4	3	2	1
(b)	1	3	4	2
(c)	2	1	3	4
(d)	3	2	4	1

31. Consider the following and identify the correct sequence of the given ranges from North to South.
I. Nallamalla Range
II. Cardamom Range
III. Vindhya Range

Codes
(a) I, III, II (b) II, III, I
(c) III, II, I (d) III, I, II

32. Identify the physical feature of India with the help of the information given below.
- This is a tableland composed of the old crystalline, igneous and metamorphic rocks.
- It was formed due to the breaking and drifting of the Gondwana land and thus, making it a part of the oldest landmass.

(a) Indian Desert
(b) Peninsular Plateau
(c) Himalayan Mountain
(d) Coastal Plains

33. Identify the mountain peaks of India marked as A and B on the map given below.

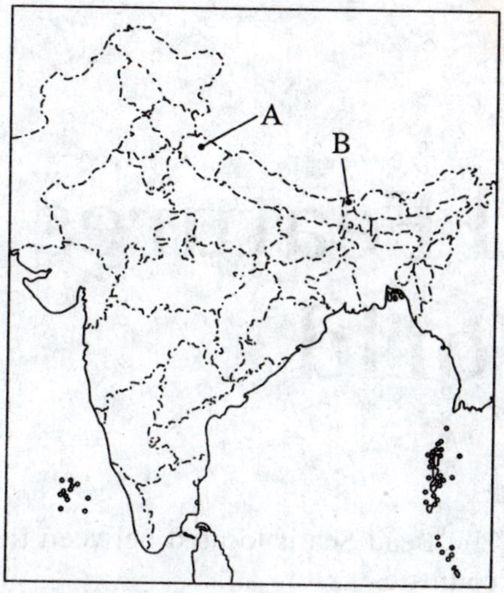

	A	B
(a)	Nanda Devi	Kangchenjunga
(b)	Amsot Peak	Kamet
(c)	Saltoro Kangri	K2
(d)	Guru Shikhar	Trishul Peak

34. There are two statements marked as Assertion (A) and Reason (R). Mark your answer as per the codes given below.

Assertion (A) The Himalayas form the highest and rugged mountains in the world.

Reason (R) The Mount Everest is the highest peak in the world lying in the Himalayas.

Codes

(a) Both A and R are true and R is the correct explanation of A

(b) Both A and R are true, but R is not the correct explanation of A

(c) A is true, but R is false

(d) A is false, but R is true

35. Read the given statements and select the option that correctly identifies true (T) and false (F) ones.

I. The Ganga-Brahmaputra Delta is the second largest delta in the world.

II. In Tibet, Brahmaputra is called Tsangpo.

III. In Himachal Pradesh, Brahmaputra is called Dihang.

Codes

	I	II	III
(a)	F	T	F
(b)	T	F	T
(c)	T	T	F
(d)	T	T	T

Darken your choice with HB Pencil

1.	ⓐ ⓑ ⓒ ⓓ	7.	ⓐ ⓑ ⓒ ⓓ	13.	ⓐ ⓑ ⓒ ⓓ	19.	ⓐ ⓑ ⓒ ⓓ	25.	ⓐ ⓑ ⓒ ⓓ	31.	ⓐ ⓑ ⓒ ⓓ
2.	ⓐ ⓑ ⓒ ⓓ	8.	ⓐ ⓑ ⓒ ⓓ	14.	ⓐ ⓑ ⓒ ⓓ	20.	ⓐ ⓑ ⓒ ⓓ	26.	ⓐ ⓑ ⓒ ⓓ	32.	ⓐ ⓑ ⓒ ⓓ
3.	ⓐ ⓑ ⓒ ⓓ	9.	ⓐ ⓑ ⓒ ⓓ	15.	ⓐ ⓑ ⓒ ⓓ	21.	ⓐ ⓑ ⓒ ⓓ	27.	ⓐ ⓑ ⓒ ⓓ	33.	ⓐ ⓑ ⓒ ⓓ
4.	ⓐ ⓑ ⓒ ⓓ	10.	ⓐ ⓑ ⓒ ⓓ	16.	ⓐ ⓑ ⓒ ⓓ	22.	ⓐ ⓑ ⓒ ⓓ	28.	ⓐ ⓑ ⓒ ⓓ	34.	ⓐ ⓑ ⓒ ⓓ
5.	ⓐ ⓑ ⓒ ⓓ	11.	ⓐ ⓑ ⓒ ⓓ	17.	ⓐ ⓑ ⓒ ⓓ	23.	ⓐ ⓑ ⓒ ⓓ	29.	ⓐ ⓑ ⓒ ⓓ	35.	ⓐ ⓑ ⓒ ⓓ
6.	ⓐ ⓑ ⓒ ⓓ	12.	ⓐ ⓑ ⓒ ⓓ	18.	ⓐ ⓑ ⓒ ⓓ	24.	ⓐ ⓑ ⓒ ⓓ	30.	ⓐ ⓑ ⓒ ⓓ		

Chapter 08

Major Physical Features of the World

MCQs 1 Mark Questions

1. Name the river which flows through London City, England.
(a) Severn (b) Thames
(c) Volga (d) None of these

2. Turkey is located between ....
(a) Black Sea and Caspian Sea
(b) Black Sea and Mediterranean Sea
(c) Gulf of Suez and Mediterranean Sea
(d) Gulf of Aqaba and Dead Sea

3. Which of the following countries does form border with Caspian Sea?
(a) Russia (b) Iran
(c) Both (a) and (b) (d) Armenia

4. The Palk Strait is located between which of the following countries?
(a) India and Sri Lanka
(b) India and Maldives
(c) India and Bangladesh
(d) India and Myanmar

5. .... desert covers a large part of the countries of Mongolia and China.
(a) Sahara (b) Gobi
(c) Kalahari (d) Thar

6. The Dead Sea is located between the two countries ....
(a) Jordan and Sudan (b) Jordan and Israel
(c) Turkey and UAE (d) UAE and Egypt

7. Identify the plateau which is known as the 'Roof of the World'.
(a) Andes (b) Himalaya
(c) Karakoram (d) Pamir

8. Which one is the largest tropical rainforest in the world?
(a) Amazon
(b) Bosawas
(c) South-East Asian Rainforest
(d) Daintree Rainforest

9. Which among the following two countries share longest land borders with each other?
(a) China and Russia
(b) USA and Canada
(c) Brazil and Argentina
(d) India and China

10. The world's largest coral reef system 'Great Barrier Reef' is located at ....
(a) India (b) Malaysia
(c) New Zealand (d) Australia

11. The Great Victoria Desert is located in which among the following countries?
(a) Canada (b) West Africa
(c) Australia (d) North America

12. Find the odd one out.
(a) Sahara Desert (b) Kalahari Desert
(c) Namib Desert (d) Gobi Desert

13. Which among the following areas is related to 'Golan Heights'?
(a) Central Asia (b) Middle East
(c) South-East Asia (d) Central Africa

14. Identify the two water bodies which are connected by the Suez Canal.
(a) Pacific Ocean and the Atlantic Ocean
(b) Sea of China with the Sea of Japan
(c) North Sea and the Baltic Sea
(d) Red Sea and the Mediterranean Sea

15. Which among the following mountains is the source of the rivers Danube and Rhine?
(a) Alps (b) Rockies
(c) Appalachians (d) Andes

16. Volcanic activity is more common in which of the following regions of the world?
(a) Japan (b) Hawai
(c) New Zealand (d) Colombia

17. Which among the following is the biggest fresh water lake in the world?
(a) Lake Assal (b) Lake Superior
(c) Lake Van (d) Dal Lake

18. .... is a river in Central Europe, the continent's second-longest after the Volga.
(a) Rhine (b) Seine (c) Thames (d) Danube

19. Name the smallest island country located in the Indian Ocean.
(a) Sri Lanka (b) Maldives
(c) Madagascar (d) Mauritius

20. The soil formed by wind dust in and around hot deserts is called ....
(a) loamy soil (b) silty soil
(c) loess soil (d) sandy soil

21. Identify the name of largest islands in the world.
(a) Borneo (b) Sumatra
(c) Greenland (d) New Guinea

22. .... sea is the world's largest inland water body.
(a) Black (b) Dead
(c) Caspian (d) Aral

23. Complete the given analogy.
Lake Victoria : Africa :: Lake Baikal : ?
(a) Africa (b) Canada
(c) United States of America (d) Russia

24. Which among the following is the second largest island in the world?
(a) Finland (b) New Guinea
(c) Borneo (d) Greenland

MCQs 2 Marks Questions

25. Consider the following countries.
I. Australia II. Namibia
III. Brazil IV. Chile Through
Which of the above countries does the Tropic of Capricorn pass?
(a) II, III and IV (b) Only I
(c) I, II, III and IV (d) I, II and III

26. Identify the physical feature of the world with the help of the information given below.
- This mountain range is located in South-Central Europe immediately North of the mediterranean sea. It is extended in France, Austria, Germany and Switzerland. Its highest peak is Mount Blanc and it is an example of young folded mountain in the world.

(a) Alps mountain range
(b) Andes mountain range
(c) Rockey mountain range
(d) Great Dividing range

27. Identify the rivers (water bodies) of the world marked as A and B on the map given below.

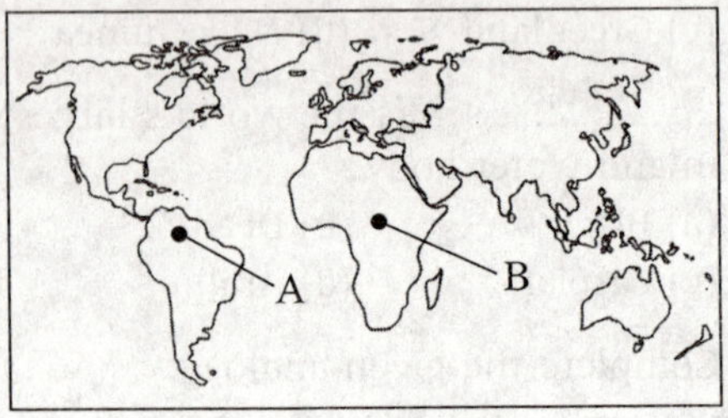

	A	B
(a)	Rhine	Danube
(b)	Amazon	Nile
(c)	Danube	Congo
(d)	Tigris	Niger

28. Match the following.

List I (Waterfalls)	**List II** (Continents)
A. Angel falls	1. Africa
B. Niagara falls	2. Asia
C. Victoria falls	3. South America
D. Jog falls	4. North America

Codes

	A	B	C	D
(a)	4	3	2	1
(b)	3	4	1	2
(c)	3	4	2	1
(d)	4	3	1	2

29. Read the given statements and select the option that correctly identifies true (T) and false (F) ones.

I. Ural mountain ranges act as a boundary between Europe and Asia.
II. Mt McKinley is the highest peak in North America.
III. River Volga is the longest river in Europe and it drains into the Caspian Sea.
IV. River Nile is the longest river in the world and originates near Lake Victoria.

Codes

	I	II	III	IV		I	II	III	IV
(a)	F	T	T	F	(b)	F	F	F	T
(c)	T	T	T	T	(d)	T	F	F	T

30. There are two statements marked as Assertion (A) and Reason (R). Mark your answer as per the codes given below.

Assertion (A) The Himalayas is a mountain range separating the plain of the Indian sub-continent from the Tibetan plateau.

Reason (R) It consists mostly of uplifted sedimentary and metamorphic rocks.

Codes

(a) Both A and R are true and R is the correct explanation of A
(b) Both A and R are true, but R is not the correct explanation of A
(c) A is true, but R is false
(d) A is false, but R is true

Darken your choice with HB Pencil

1. ⓐ ⓑ ⓒ ⓓ	6. ⓐ ⓑ ⓒ ⓓ	11. ⓐ ⓑ ⓒ ⓓ	16. ⓐ ⓑ ⓒ ⓓ	21. ⓐ ⓑ ⓒ ⓓ	26. ⓐ ⓑ ⓒ ⓓ
2. ⓐ ⓑ ⓒ ⓓ	7. ⓐ ⓑ ⓒ ⓓ	12. ⓐ ⓑ ⓒ ⓓ	17. ⓐ ⓑ ⓒ ⓓ	22. ⓐ ⓑ ⓒ ⓓ	27. ⓐ ⓑ ⓒ ⓓ
3. ⓐ ⓑ ⓒ ⓓ	8. ⓐ ⓑ ⓒ ⓓ	13. ⓐ ⓑ ⓒ ⓓ	18. ⓐ ⓑ ⓒ ⓓ	23. ⓐ ⓑ ⓒ ⓓ	28. ⓐ ⓑ ⓒ ⓓ
4. ⓐ ⓑ ⓒ ⓓ	9. ⓐ ⓑ ⓒ ⓓ	14. ⓐ ⓑ ⓒ ⓓ	19. ⓐ ⓑ ⓒ ⓓ	24. ⓐ ⓑ ⓒ ⓓ	29. ⓐ ⓑ ⓒ ⓓ
5. ⓐ ⓑ ⓒ ⓓ	10. ⓐ ⓑ ⓒ ⓓ	15. ⓐ ⓑ ⓒ ⓓ	20. ⓐ ⓑ ⓒ ⓓ	25. ⓐ ⓑ ⓒ ⓓ	30. ⓐ ⓑ ⓒ ⓓ

Chapter 09

Forests and Wildlife Resources of India

MCQs 1 Mark Questions

1. Bandipur National Park is located in which of the following states?
(a) Andhra Pradesh (b) Rajasthan
(c) Assam (d) Karnataka

2. Which among the following was the first national park established in India?
(a) Kanha National Park
(b) Valmiki National Park
(c) Dudhwa National Park
(d) Jim Corbett National Park

3. Which one of the following states has the largest area under permanent forests?
(a) Bihar (b) Kerala
(c) Madhya Pradesh (d) Uttar Pradesh

4. Identify the incorrectly matched pair.

National Park		Location
(a) Sariska	–	Rajasthan
(b) Jim Corbett	–	Uttarakhand
(c) Kanha	–	Jharkhand
(d) Gir	–	Gujarat

5. Biosphere Reserve of India Nanda Devi (UNESCO) is located in the state of ....
(a) Meghalaya (b) Himachal Pradesh
(c) Sikkim (d) Uttarakhand

6. The famous Chipko Movement was started by Amrita Devi in .... to protect trees from being cut.
(a) 1973 (b) 1965
(c) 1985 (d) 1975

7. In which one of the following states is the Gulf of Mannar National Park located?
(a) Jharkhand
(b) Tamil Nadu
(c) Chhattisgarh
(d) Odisha

8. Which type of forests are found in Gujarat and Rajasthan?
(a) Montane Forests
(b) Thorn Forests and Scrubs
(c) Tropical Evergreen Forests
(d) Mangrove Forests

9. Complete the given analogy.
Project Tiger : 1972 :: Project Elephant : ?
(a) 1992 (b) 1982
(c) 1975 (d) 1987

10. Which among the following forests are also called monsoon forests?
(a) The Thorn Forests and Scrubs
(b) Tropical Evergreen Forests
(c) Tropical Deciduous Forests
(d) Montane Forests

11. The deltas of the Ganga, the Mahanadi, the Krishna, the Godavari, and the Kaveri are covered by ....
(a) Mangrove Forests
(b) Montane Forests
(c) Tropical Deciduous Forests
(d) Tropical Thorn Forests and Scrubs

12. Royal Bengal Tiger is the famous animal of which of the following forests?
(a) Tropical Deciduous Forests
(b) Tropical Thorn Forests and Scrubs
(c) Montane Forests
(d) Mangrove Forests

13. The leaves of which tree are used as a cure for eye sores?
(a) Arjun (b) Babool (c) Neem (d) Tulsi

14. Which one of the following trees is abundant in the temperate zone of the Western Himalayas?
(a) Blue pine (b) Silver fur
(c) Deodar (d) Pine

15. Identify the correctly matched pair.

Wildlife Sanctuary		State
(a) Ranthambore	–	Rajasthan
(b) Similipal	–	Bihar
(c) Manas	–	Uttar Pradesh
(d) Pench	–	Tamil Nadu

16. Which of the following national parks is the natural habitat of the Indian lion ?
(a) Gir National Park
(b) Manas National Park
(c) Kaziranga National Park
(d) Bandhavgarh National Park

17. Complete the given analogy.
Uttarakhand : Jim Corbett National Park :: Kerala : ?
(a) Periyar National Park
(b) Similipal National Park
(c) Kanha National Park
(d) Chandra Prabha National Park

18. Which among the following trees has high antibiotic and antibacterial properties?
(a) Neem (b) Tulsi
(c) Jamun (d) Sarpagandha

MCQs 2 Marks Questions

19. Consider the following statements and choose the correct option.
I. India has 18 biosphere reserves.
II. There are 106 national parks, 567 wildlife sanctuaries and zoological gardens in India.

Codes
(a) Only I (b) Only II
(c) Both I and II (d) Neither I nor II

20. Match the following.

List I (Types of Forest)	List II (Tree)
A. Tropical Evergreen Forests	1. Mahogany
B. Tropical Deciduous Forests	2. Teak
C. Tropical Thorn Forests and Scrubs	3. Acacias
D. Montane Forests	4. Deodar

Codes

	A	B	C	D		A	B	C	D
(a)	1	2	3	4	(b)	4	3	2	1
(c)	2	4	1	3	(d)	3	1	4	2

21. Consider the following statments is correct regarding the Himalayan yew?
I. It is rare animal species.
II. It is under threat due to over-exploitation.
III. It is found in Himachal Pradesh and Arunachal Pradesh.

Codes
(a) Only I (b) Only II
(c) II and III (d) All of these

22. Read the given statements regarding Tropical Evergreen Forests and select the option that correctly identifies true (T) and false (F) ones.

I. These are found in the Western Ghats and the island groups of Lakshadweep, Andaman and Nicobar, upper parts of Assam and Tamil Nadu coast.

II. The trees reach great heights up to 60 metres or even above.

III. The common animals found in these forests are elephants, monkeys, lemurs, and deer.

Code

	I	II	III		I	II	III
(a)	T	F	F	(b)	F	T	T
(c)	T	T	F	(d)	T	T	T

23. Identify the type of forests with the help of the information given below.

- This type of vegetation is found in the North-Western part of the country, including semi-arid areas of Gujarat, Rajasthan, Madhya Pradesh, Chhattisgarh, Uttar Pradesh, and Haryana.
- Acacias, palms, euphorbias, and cacti are the main plant species.

(a) Tropical Deciduous Forests
(b) Tropical Thorn Forests and Scrubs
(c) Mangrove Forests
(d) Dry Deciduous Forests

24. There are two statements marked as Assertion (A) and Reason (R). Mark your answer as per the codes given below.

Assertion (A) Manas National Park is located in two districts of Assam and it is situated at the foothills of the Himalayas.

Reason (R) River Manas, a major tributary of the Brahmaputra, divides this national park into two halves and forms a border with Bhutan.

Codes

(a) Both A and R are true and R is the correct explanation of A
(b) Both A and R are true, but R is not the correct explanation of A
(c) A is true, but R is false
(d) A is false, but R is true

25. Identify the national park which is marked as A on the given map of India.

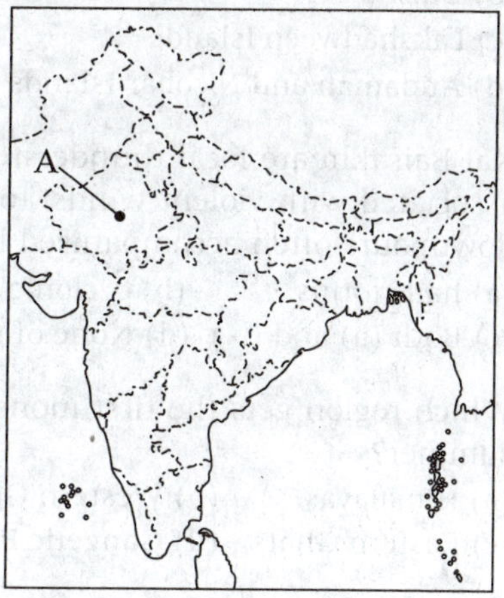

(a) Similipal National Park
(b) Buxa National Park
(c) Gir National Park
(d) Ranthambore National Park

Darken your choice with HB Pencil

1.	a b c d	6.	a b c d	11.	a b c d	16.	a b c d	21.	a b c d
2.	a b c d	7.	a b c d	12.	a b c d	17.	a b c d	22.	a b c d
3.	a b c d	8.	a b c d	13.	a b c d	18.	a b c d	23.	a b c d
4.	a b c d	9.	a b c d	14.	a b c d	19.	a b c d	24.	a b c d
5.	a b c d	10.	a b c d	15.	a b c d	20.	a b c d	25.	a b c d

Chapter 10

Weather and Climate

MCQs 1 Mark Questions

1. Which part of India receives rainfall from both the South-West and North-West monsoons?
   (a) Tamil Nadu
   (b) Odisha
   (c) Lakshadweep Islands
   (d) Andaman and Nicobar Islands

2. Kal Baisakhi are local thunderstorms associated with violent winds, torrential downpours often accompanised by ....
   (a) hail storms (b) cyclonic storms
   (c) Both (a) and (b) (d) None of these

3. Which region gets the first monsoon in summer?
   (a) Himalayas (b) Western Ghats
   (c) Eastern Ghats (d) Gangetic Plains

4. Identify the element(s) which affect the weather and climate.
   (a) Atmospheric pressure
   (b) Humidity
   (c) Temperature
   (d) All of the above

5. The pre-monsoon mango showers occur pre-dominantly in ....
   (a) West Bengal and Assam
   (b) Deccan Plateau
   (c) Gujarat and Maharashtra
   (d) Kerala and Karnataka

6. Which of the following states receives rainfall due to Western disturbances?
   (a) Punjab (b) West Bengal
   (c) Kerala (d) Gujarat

7. The North-Eastern hills that block the South-West monsoon winds and cause heavy rains in Assam are ....
   (a) Arakan Yoma and Pegu Yoma
   (b) Garo Khasi and Jaintia Hills
   (c) Barail and Patkai Hills
   (d) Khasi and Pegu Yoma

8. Which one of the following states receives the highest rainfall during winter months?
   (a) Punjab (b) Kerala
   (c) Meghalaya (d) Tamil Nadu

9. Monsoon originates by which of the following winds in India?
   (a) South-West winds
   (b) South-East Winds
   (c) North-East winds
   (d) North-West winds

10. The main cause of global climatic change is ....
    (a) an increase in the content of carbon dioxide in the atmosphere
    (b) emissions of industrial gases
    (c) adding of the dust
    (d) changes in plant cover

11. Which one of the following places receives the highest rainfall in the world?
(a) Guwahati
(b) Mawsynram
(c) Silchar
(d) Agartala

12. Which one of the following places has the maximum rainfall?
(a) Cochin
(b) Cherrapunji
(c) Guwahati
(d) Panaji

13. The South-West monsoon blows during ....
(a) October-December
(b) June-September
(c) November-January
(d) None of the above

14. Which one of the following places has the lowest annual rainfall?
(a) Kutch (b) Leh
(c) Bellary (d) Jodhpur

15. India gets maximum rainfall mainly from ....
(a) retreating monsoon
(b) convectional rainfall
(c) North-East monsoon
(d) South-West monsoon

16. Why do coastal areas experience less contrast in temperature conditions?
(a) Due to moderating effect of the seas
(b) Due to landmass
(c) Due to heat conditions
(d) None of the above

17. The state of the atmosphere over an area at any point of time is known as ....
(a) weather (b) climate
(c) heat (d) cold

18. Arrange the seasons in the correct chronological order as they occur in India.
(a) Rainy, Summer, Autumn, Spring
(b) Spring, Summer, Rainy, Autumn
(c) Rainy, Autumn, Spring, Summer
(d) Summer, Spring, Rainy, Autumn

19. Delhi gets winter rainfall due to ....
(a) South-West monsoon
(b) North-East monsoon
(c) conventional rain
(d) Western disturbances

MCQs 2 Marks Questions

20. Which of the following is/are correct about declining of monsoon?
I. Clear sky
II. Pressure condition in Bay of Bengal
III. Rising temperature of land

Codes
(a) Only I
(b) Only II
(c) Both II and III
(d) All of the above

21. There are two statements marked as Assertion (A) and Reason (R). Mark your answer as per the codes given below.

Assertion (A) Northern plains of India receive some rainfall in winter.

Reason (R) North-East monsoon is active in winter.

Codes
(a) Both A and R are true, but R is not the correct explanation of A
(b) A is false, but R is true
(c) Both A and R are true and R is the correct explanation of A
(d) A is true, but R is false

22. Consider the following statements and choose the correct option.

I. Tamil Nadu is located in South-East peninsula India.

II. Tamil Nadu receives about 50-60% of its annual rainfall during North-East monsoon.

Codes

(a) Only I (b) Only II
(c) Both I and II (d) Neither I nor II

23. Identify the type of climate with the help of the information given below.

It is a seasonal change in the direction of the prevailing or strongest winds of a region. It causes wet and dry seasons throughout much of the tropics. It is most often associated with the Indian Ocean.

(a) Monsoon climate (b) Spring climate
(c) Summer climate (d) Winter climate

24. Match the following terms with what they measure/indicate.

List I	List II
A. Hygrometer	1. Atmospheric pressure
B. Barometer	2. Humidity
C. Wind vane	3. Wind speed
D. Anemometer	4. Wind direction

Codes

	A	B	C	D
(a)	2	1	4	3
(b)	3	2	1	4
(c)	1	2	4	3
(d)	2	3	4	1

25. Which of the following are the main reasons for the origin of the South-West monsoon in India?

I. Development of low pressure in North-West India.

II. Deflection of trade winds.

III. Arrival of the cyclonic stream from the Pacific Ocean.

Codes

(a) I and III (b) I and II
(c) II and III (d) Only III

26. Identify the monsoon winds as marked on the map given below.

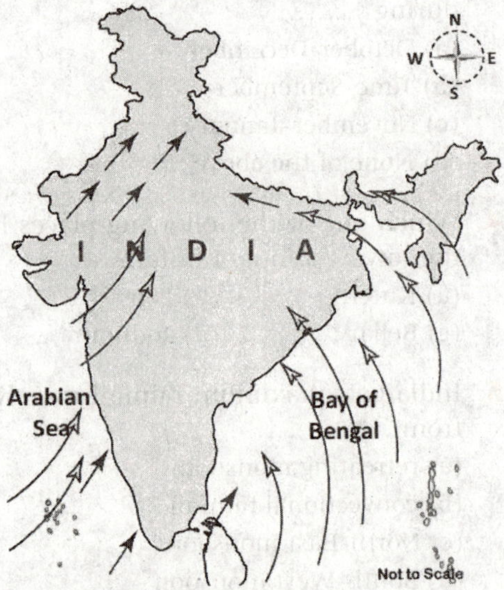

(a) South-West monsoon
(b) North-East monsoon
(c) Western disturbances
(d) North-West monsoon

Darken your choice with HB Pencil

1.	ⓐ ⓑ ⓒ ⓓ	6.	ⓐ ⓑ ⓒ ⓓ	11.	ⓐ ⓑ ⓒ ⓓ	16.	ⓐ ⓑ ⓒ ⓓ	21.	ⓐ ⓑ ⓒ ⓓ	26.	ⓐ ⓑ ⓒ ⓓ
2.	ⓐ ⓑ ⓒ ⓓ	7.	ⓐ ⓑ ⓒ ⓓ	12.	ⓐ ⓑ ⓒ ⓓ	17.	ⓐ ⓑ ⓒ ⓓ	22.	ⓐ ⓑ ⓒ ⓓ		
3.	ⓐ ⓑ ⓒ ⓓ	8.	ⓐ ⓑ ⓒ ⓓ	13.	ⓐ ⓑ ⓒ ⓓ	18.	ⓐ ⓑ ⓒ ⓓ	23.	ⓐ ⓑ ⓒ ⓓ		
4.	ⓐ ⓑ ⓒ ⓓ	9.	ⓐ ⓑ ⓒ ⓓ	14.	ⓐ ⓑ ⓒ ⓓ	19.	ⓐ ⓑ ⓒ ⓓ	24.	ⓐ ⓑ ⓒ ⓓ		
5.	ⓐ ⓑ ⓒ ⓓ	10.	ⓐ ⓑ ⓒ ⓓ	15.	ⓐ ⓑ ⓒ ⓓ	20.	ⓐ ⓑ ⓒ ⓓ	25.	ⓐ ⓑ ⓒ ⓓ		

Chapter 11

Continents

MCQs 1 Mark Questions

1. The continent through which both the Tropic of Cancer and the Tropic of Capricorn pass is ....
(a) North America
(b) Asia
(c) Africa
(d) Europe

2. Equator passes through which of the following countries in African continent?
(a) Cameroon
(b) Costa Rica
(c) Kenya
(d) Venezuela

3. Which of the following two countries are separated by the McMahon line?
(a) India and Pakistan
(b) India and Bangladesh
(c) India and China
(d) India and Afghanistan

4. Name the continent of the world that does not have any desert.
(a) Australia
(b) Europe
(c) Asia
(d) North America

5. Which among the following deserts does not belong to the Asia continent?
(a) Arabia
(b) Gobi
(c) Sahara
(d) Thar

6. .... is the highest mountain on the African continent. It is located in Tanzania.
(a) Mount Elbrus
(b) Mount Elgon
(c) Mount Kenya
(d) Mount Kilimanjaro

7. The Kalahari Desert is located in which among the following continents?
(a) Africa
(b) Asia
(c) Europe
(d) South America

8. Identify the continents that form a mirror image of each other.
(a) North America and South America
(b) Asia and Africa
(c) Africa and South America
(d) Europe and Asia

9. Asia continent is located in which of the following hemispheres of the Earth?
(a) Eastern and Northern Hemisphere
(b) Western and Northern Hemisphere
(c) Southern and Northern Hemisphere
(d) Northern Hemisphere

10. Identify the imaginary line that passes through Asia.
(a) Equator, Tropic of Cancer and Arctic Circle
(b) Equator, Tropic of Capricorn and Arctic Circle
(c) International Date line and Tropic of Capricorn
(d) International Date line, Tropic of Cancer and Arctic Circle

11. Which of the following separates Asia from the African continent?
(a) Berling Strait and the Red Sea
(b) Red Sea and Arabian Sea
(c) Suez Canal and Red Sea
(d) Suez Canal and Berling Strait

12. Complete the given analogy.
Australia : The smallest continent : : ? : The largest continent
(a) Asia
(b) Australia
(c) North America
(d) South America

13. Which continent is known as the continent of superlatives?
(a) Europe (b) Asia
(c) Australia (d) Antarctica

14. Name the continent which is known as the Peninsula of Peninsulas.
(a) Europe (b) Asia
(c) Australia (d) South America

15. Which continent has the maximum number of countries?
(a) North America
(b) South America
(c) Asia
(d) Africa

16. The Mississippi River flows in which continent?
(a) South America
(b) Asia
(c) Europe
(d) North America

17. Angel Falls, is the world's highest uninterrupted waterfall, with a height of 979 meters is located in ....
(a) South America
(b) Asia
(c) Europe
(d) North America

18. Name the Southernmost tip of the African continent.
(a) Cape Blanco
(b) Cape Agulhas
(c) Cape of Good Hope
(d) Cape Town

19. Which is the longest river in Asian continent?
(a) Ganga River
(b) Yantze River
(c) Mekong River
(d) Yellow River

20. Which continent includes the United Kingdom, France and Germany?
(a) South America
(b) Asia
(c) Europe
(d) North America

21. Identify the continent, which is known as a continent of contrast.

(a) Europe (b) Asia
(c) Australia (d) South America

22. The Mount Everest is the highest mountain of the world, located in which of the following continents?

(a) Australia (b) Africa
(c) Asia (d) North America

23. Which of the following continents has no active volcanic regions?

(a) North America
(b) Europe
(c) Africa
(d) Australia

24. Which among the following continents surrounded by Pacific Ocean in the East and Atlantic Ocean in the West?

(a) South America
(b) Asia
(c) Europe
(d) North America

25. Identify the incorrectly matched pair.

Deepest Point		Continent
(a) Assal Lake	–	Africa
(b) Dead Sea	–	Asia
(c) Death Valley	–	South America
(d) Caspian Sea	–	Europe

MCQs 2 Marks Questions

26. Consider the following statements and choose the correct option.

I. A continent is a large continuous mass of land convectionally regarded as a collective region.
II. There are seven major landmasses or continents on the Earth.
III. Africa is the second largest continent of the world.

Codes

(a) Both I and II
(b) Both II and III
(c) Only III
(d) All of the above

27. Identify the continent of the world with the help of the information given below.

- It is the seventh largest continent in the world.
- It is also known as 'the island continent' as it is surrounded by the ocean.

(a) Australia
(b) Asia
(c) North America
(d) South America

28. There are two statements marked as Assertion (A) and Reason (R). Mark your answer as per the codes given below.

Assertion (A) Antarctica is the Southernmost and fifth largest continent in the world.

Reason (R) The climate of Antarctica is freezing cold, because of its distance from the Equator.

Codes

(a) Both A and R are true and R is the correct explanation of A
(b) Both A and R are true, but R is not the correct explanation of A
(c) A is true, but R is false
(d) A is false, but R is true

29. Read the given statements regarding continent and select the option that correctly identifies true (T) and false (F) ones.

I. The continent of Antarctica is located in Northern Hemisphere.

II. The continent of Antarctica is called as the white continent.

III. The continent of Australia is called the land of Golden Fleece.

Codes

	I	II	III		I	II	III
(a)	T	F	F	(b)	F	T	T
(c)	T	T	F	(d)	T	T	T

30. Match the following.

List I (Mountains)	**List II** (Continents)
A. Atlas	1. North America
B. Appalachian	2. Africa
C. Hindukush	3. Asia
D. Andes	4. South America

Codes

	A	B	C	D
(a)	2	1	3	4
(b)	4	1	3	2
(c)	1	2	3	4
(d)	4	3	1	2

31. Consider the following statements and choose the correct option.

I. The Alps are the highest and most extensive mountain range system that lies entirely in Europe.

II. Europe lies to the East of Asia and it is bounded by water bodies on three sides.

Codes

(a) Both I and II

(b) Only I

(c) Only II

(d) None of the above

Darken your choice with HB Pencil

1. ⓐ ⓑ ⓒ ⓓ	7. ⓐ ⓑ ⓒ ⓓ	13. ⓐ ⓑ ⓒ ⓓ	19. ⓐ ⓑ ⓒ ⓓ	25. ⓐ ⓑ ⓒ ⓓ	31. ⓐ ⓑ ⓒ ⓓ
2. ⓐ ⓑ ⓒ ⓓ	8. ⓐ ⓑ ⓒ ⓓ	14. ⓐ ⓑ ⓒ ⓓ	20. ⓐ ⓑ ⓒ ⓓ	26. ⓐ ⓑ ⓒ ⓓ	
3. ⓐ ⓑ ⓒ ⓓ	9. ⓐ ⓑ ⓒ ⓓ	15. ⓐ ⓑ ⓒ ⓓ	21. ⓐ ⓑ ⓒ ⓓ	27. ⓐ ⓑ ⓒ ⓓ	
4. ⓐ ⓑ ⓒ ⓓ	10. ⓐ ⓑ ⓒ ⓓ	16. ⓐ ⓑ ⓒ ⓓ	22. ⓐ ⓑ ⓒ ⓓ	28. ⓐ ⓑ ⓒ ⓓ	
5. ⓐ ⓑ ⓒ ⓓ	11. ⓐ ⓑ ⓒ ⓓ	17. ⓐ ⓑ ⓒ ⓓ	23. ⓐ ⓑ ⓒ ⓓ	29. ⓐ ⓑ ⓒ ⓓ	
6. ⓐ ⓑ ⓒ ⓓ	12. ⓐ ⓑ ⓒ ⓓ	18. ⓐ ⓑ ⓒ ⓓ	24. ⓐ ⓑ ⓒ ⓓ	30. ⓐ ⓑ ⓒ ⓓ	

Chapter 12

Ecology and Environment

MCQs 1 Mark Questions

1. Which of the following gases are called greenhouse gases?
(a) Methane (b) Nitrogen
(c) Carbon dioxide (d) Both (a) and (c)

2. Biotic component of environment includes ....
(a) land (b) air
(c) plants (d) water

3. In a food chain, the total amount of living material is depicted by ....
(a) pyramid of biomass
(b) pyramid of energy
(c) pyramid of number
(d) tropic levels

4. Which of the following can act as the top consumer in a grassland ecosystem?
(a) Carnivores
(b) Herbivores
(c) Either carnivores or herbivores
(d) Bacteria

5. Which of the following has coined the term 'ecology' for the first time?
(a) Linnaeus (b) William
(c) Odum (d) Haeckel

6. The World Wildlife Fund (WWF) is one of the largest conservation organisations in the world. Which of the following animals is the symbol of WWF?
(a) Dodo (b) Giant Panda
(c) Bison (d) Bengal Tiger

7. Bhopal gas tragedy was caused by which gas?
(a) Ethyl isocyanate
(b) Methyl isocyanate
(c) Carbon monoxide
(d) Sulphur dioxide and nitrous oxide

8. Smoke, fumes, ash, dust, nitric oxide and sulphur dioxide are the main sources of ....
(a) primary pollutants
(b) secondary pollutants
(c) bio-degradable pollutants
(d) None of the above

9. The noise intensity is measured in which of the following measuring units?
(a) Hertz (b) Decibel
(c) Dobson (d) Metre/Second

10. Identify the agent which is responsible for turning the Taj Mahal yellow.
(a) Sulphur (b) Chlorine
(c) Sulphur dioxide (d) Nitrogen dioxide

11. Which of the following pollutants is/are responsible for the causes of smog?
(a) Nitrogen oxides
(b) Emission from vehicles
(c) Volatile organic compounds
(d) All of the above

12. Which of the following is called the secondary air pollutant?
(a) PANs (b) Ozone
(c) Carbon monoxide (d) Nitrogen dioxide

13. Complete the given analogy.
Ex-situ site : ? : : In-situ site : National Park
(a) Sacred Groves (b) Wildlife Sanctuary
(c) Seed Bank (d) National Park

14. .... is one of the most prevalent hotspots of biodiversity in India.
(a) Himalayas (b) Western Ghats
(c) Ganges (d) None of these

15. Identify the name of units which is used for measuring ozone thickness.
(a) Dobson (b) Pascal
(c) Decibel (d) Light year

16. Which of the following instruments is used to measure the intensity of an earthquake?
(a) Richter scale (b) Seismograph
(c) Modified Mercalli scale (d) Hydrograph

17. Which among the following regions has maximum biodiversity?
(a) Temperate Rainforest
(b) Taiga
(c) Tropical Rainforest
(d) Mangroves

18. Which of the following ecosystems has highest bio-mass?
(a) Desert Ecosystem
(b) Freshwater Ecosystem
(c) Tundra Ecosystem
(d) Forest Ecosystem

19. What is the ecological system integrating all living beings and their relationships called?
(a) Total Wildlife (b) Biosphere
(c) Lithosphere (d) Hydrosphere

20. Biological indicator of pollution of sulphur dioxide is ....
(a) moss (b) smoke
(c) bryophyte (d) None of these

21. What is the name of the feature that allows organisms to survive in the conditions of their habitat?
(a) Adjustment (b) Adaptation
(c) Acclimatisation (d) Adaptive variation

22. Two biodiversity hotspots in India are ....
(a) Eastern Himalayas and Western Ghats
(b) Eastern Ghats and Western Ghats
(c) Eastern Himalayas and Eastern Ghats
(d) Western Himalayas and Eastern Ghats

MCQs 2 Marks Questions

23. The biosphere is a region of the Earth which supports life. It includes
I. Hydrosphere II. Lithosphere
III. Stratosphere IV. Troposphere
Codes
(a) Both I and III (b) I, II and IV
(c) Both I and IV (d) II, III and IV

24. Identify the environmental factor with the help of the information given below.
- It is the phenomenon of a gradual increase in the average temperature of the Earth's atmosphere and its water bodies.
- The leading cause for this environmental issue is the increased volumes of greenhouse gases, in the atmosphere, mainly from human activities such as burning fossil fuel, farming, etc.

(a) Global warming
(b) Solid waste pollution
(c) Deforestation
(d) Climate change

25. Match the following.

List I (Components)	List II (Related to)
A. Biosphere	1. Blanket of air which surrounds the Earth
B. Atmosphere	2. Narrow zone where land, water and air interact
C. Hydrosphere	3. Domain of water
D. Environment	4. Our surroundings

Codes

	A	B	C	D		A	B	C	D
(a)	2	1	3	4	(b)	3	2	1	4
(c)	1	2	4	3	(d)	2	3	4	1

26. There are two statements marked as Assertion (A) and Reason (R). Mark your answer as per the codes given below.

Assertion (A) Biodiversity maintains the ecosystem by maintaining the food chain.

Reason (R) Biodiversity help in scientific research, education and monitoring. For example, research about new genetic materials with the help of gene pools.

Codes

(a) Both A and R are true, but R is not the correct explanation of A
(b) A is false, but R is true
(c) Both A and R are true and R is the correct explanation of A
(d) A is true, but R is false

27. Consider the following statements and choose the correct option.

I. A mangrove is a shrub or small tree that grows in coastal saline or brackish water.

II. Scavengers are animals that Feed on dead and decaying Plants and animals.

Codes

(a) Only I (b) Only II
(c) Both I and II (d) None of these

28. Identify the national park located in Indian state as marked on the map given below.

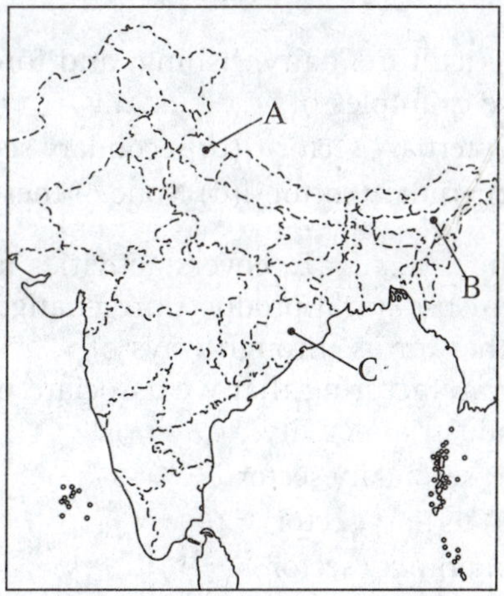

	A	B	C
(a)	Rajaji	Manas	Buxa
(b)	Jim Corbett	Kaziranga	Similipal
(c)	Jim Corbett	Buxa	Similipal
(d)	Rajaji	Kaziranga	Buxa

Darken your choice with HB Pencil

1. ⓐ ⓑ ⓒ ⓓ	6. ⓐ ⓑ ⓒ ⓓ	11. ⓐ ⓑ ⓒ ⓓ	16. ⓐ ⓑ ⓒ ⓓ	21. ⓐ ⓑ ⓒ ⓓ	26. ⓐ ⓑ ⓒ ⓓ
2. ⓐ ⓑ ⓒ ⓓ	7. ⓐ ⓑ ⓒ ⓓ	12. ⓐ ⓑ ⓒ ⓓ	17. ⓐ ⓑ ⓒ ⓓ	22. ⓐ ⓑ ⓒ ⓓ	27. ⓐ ⓑ ⓒ ⓓ
3. ⓐ ⓑ ⓒ ⓓ	8. ⓐ ⓑ ⓒ ⓓ	13. ⓐ ⓑ ⓒ ⓓ	18. ⓐ ⓑ ⓒ ⓓ	23. ⓐ ⓑ ⓒ ⓓ	28. ⓐ ⓑ ⓒ ⓓ
4. ⓐ ⓑ ⓒ ⓓ	9. ⓐ ⓑ ⓒ ⓓ	14. ⓐ ⓑ ⓒ ⓓ	19. ⓐ ⓑ ⓒ ⓓ	24. ⓐ ⓑ ⓒ ⓓ	
5. ⓐ ⓑ ⓒ ⓓ	10. ⓐ ⓑ ⓒ ⓓ	15. ⓐ ⓑ ⓒ ⓓ	20. ⓐ ⓑ ⓒ ⓓ	25. ⓐ ⓑ ⓒ ⓓ	

Chapter 13

Sectors of Indian Economy

MCQs 1 Mark Questions

1. Agriculture, dairy, fishing, and forestry are examples of ....
   (a) tertiary sector (b) secondary sector
   (c) primary sector (d) None of these

2. The .... covers activities in which natural products are changed into other forms through ways of manufacturing that we associate with industrial activity.
   (a) secondary sector
   (b) tertiary sector
   (c) primary sector
   (d) None of the above

3. Which of the following comes under the tertiary sector?
   (a) Transport
   (b) Communication
   (c) Both (a) and (b)
   (d) None of the above

4. Complete the given analogy.
   Primary sector : ? :: Secondary sector : Construction
   (a) Mining
   (b) Real estate
   (c) Financial service
   (d) Electricity

5. Which sector contributed the maximum to GDP at the time of independence?
   (a) Services (b) Agriculture
   (c) Manufacturing (d) None of these

6. Which sector has emerged as the largest producing sector in India?
   (a) Secondary sector
   (b) Tertiary sector
   (c) Primary sector
   (d) Science and Technology sector

7. Which among the following is an activity performed by tertiary sectors?
   (a) Studying in college
   (b) Transporting goods
   (c) Manufacturing clothes
   (d) Working on farms

8. Identify the incorrectly matched pair.
   (a) Primary occupation – Quarrying
   (b) Secondary occupation – Refining
   (c) Tertiary occupation – Communication
   (d) None of the above

9. Which type of unemployment occurs when people cannot find jobs during some months of the year?
   (a) Structural unemployment
   (b) Cyclical unemployment
   (c) Seasonal unemployment
   (d) None of the above

10. Which unemployment occurs when the number of persons working on a farm is more than required?
(a) Cyclic unemployment
(b) Disguised unemployment
(c) Structural unemployment
(d) Frictional unemployment

11. Identify the correct statement(s) regarding the unorganised sector.
(a) This sector includes a large number of people who are employed on their own doing small jobs.
(b) Employment is not secure.
(c) People can be asked to leave without any reason.
(d) All of the above

12. The sector where government owns most of the assets and provides all the services is known as ....
(a) private sector (b) public sector
(c) organised sector (d) tertiary sector

13. The unemployment which exists in any economy due to people being in the process of moving from one job to another is known as ....
(a) seasonal unemployment
(b) cyclic unemployment
(c) frictional unemployment
(d) structural unemployment

14. What is the value of all final goods and services produced within a country during a particular year called?
(a) Gross Domestic Product
(b) Net Domestic Product
(c) National Product
(d) Production of Tertiary Sector

15. Which sector contributes the most income to India's economy?
(a) Primary sector (b) Secondary sector
(c) Tertiary sector (d) None of these

16. Which among the following continues to be the largest employer in India?
(a) Quaternary sector
(b) Tertiary sector
(c) Secondary sector
(d) Primary sector

17. Information and communication technology is associated with ....
(a) primary sector (b) secondary sector
(c) tertiary sector (d) None of these

18. Which one of the following economic activities is not in the tertiary sector?
(a) Banking
(b) Bee keeping
(c) Teaching
(d) Working in a call centre

19. The unorganised sector is characterised by small and scattered units which are largely outside the control of the ....
(a) employers (b) private individuals
(c) government (d) employees

20. Which of the following statements is/are true regarding the organised sector?
(a) Workers in the organised sector enjoy the security of employment.
(b) They are expected to work only a fixed number of hours.
(c) If they work more, they have to be paid overtime by the employer.
(d) All of the above

21. When we produce a goods by exploiting natural resources, it is called ....
(a) primary sector (b) service sector
(c) public sector (d) tertiary sector

22. Arrange the various sectors in the descending order based on their contribution to India's GDP.
(a) Primary sector, Secondary sector, Tertiary sector

(b) Primary sector, Tertiary sector, Secondary sector
(c) Tertiary sector, Secondary sector, Primary sector
(d) Secondary sector, Tertiary sector, Primary sector

23. Identify the sector of economy on the basis of the pictures given below.

(a) Secondary sector (b) Tertiary sector
(c) Primary sector (d) Quaternary sector

MCQs 2 Marks Questions

24. Match the following.

List I (Sectors)	List II (Activities)
A. Non-Economic activity	1. Construction of a building
B. Primary activity	2. Doctor treating patients
C. Secondary activity	3. Cooking for family
D. Tertiary activity	4. Fisherman catching fish

Codes

	A	B	C	D		A	B	C	D
(a)	3	4	1	2	(b)	1	4	2	3
(c)	4	1	3	2	(d)	2	3	1	4

25. Consider the following statements and choose the correct option.

I. The growth of secondary sector spread its influence during the Industrial Revolution in the 19th century.

II. People engaged in primary activities are called red-collar workers due to the outdoor nature of their work.

Codes

(a) Only I (b) Only II
(c) Both I and II (d) Neither I nor II

26. Read the given statements and select the option that correctly identifies true (T) and false (F) ones.

I. Service sector also includes some essential services that may not directly help in the production of goods.

II. A large proportion of labourers in India are working in the unorganised sector.

III. Disguised unemployment is a form of underemployment where one has a job but the work is divided.

Codes

	I	II	III		I	II	III
(a)	T	T	T	(b)	F	T	T
(c)	T	T	F	(d)	F	F	T

27. Identify the sector of Indian economy with the help of the information given below.

- It includes the industries where finished products are made from natural materials produced in the primary sector.
- This sector is associated with different kinds of industries. Thus, it is also called industrial sector.

(a) Secondary sector (b) Tertiary sector
(c) Primary sector (d) Quaternary sector

Darken your choice with HB Pencil

1.	ⓐ ⓑ ⓒ ⓓ	6.	ⓐ ⓑ ⓒ ⓓ	11.	ⓐ ⓑ ⓒ ⓓ	16.	ⓐ ⓑ ⓒ ⓓ	21.	ⓐ ⓑ ⓒ ⓓ	26.	ⓐ ⓑ ⓒ ⓓ
2.	ⓐ ⓑ ⓒ ⓓ	7.	ⓐ ⓑ ⓒ ⓓ	12.	ⓐ ⓑ ⓒ ⓓ	17.	ⓐ ⓑ ⓒ ⓓ	22.	ⓐ ⓑ ⓒ ⓓ	27.	ⓐ ⓑ ⓒ ⓓ
3.	ⓐ ⓑ ⓒ ⓓ	8.	ⓐ ⓑ ⓒ ⓓ	13.	ⓐ ⓑ ⓒ ⓓ	18.	ⓐ ⓑ ⓒ ⓓ	23.	ⓐ ⓑ ⓒ ⓓ		
4.	ⓐ ⓑ ⓒ ⓓ	9.	ⓐ ⓑ ⓒ ⓓ	14.	ⓐ ⓑ ⓒ ⓓ	19.	ⓐ ⓑ ⓒ ⓓ	24.	ⓐ ⓑ ⓒ ⓓ		
5.	ⓐ ⓑ ⓒ ⓓ	10.	ⓐ ⓑ ⓒ ⓓ	15.	ⓐ ⓑ ⓒ ⓓ	20.	ⓐ ⓑ ⓒ ⓓ	25.	ⓐ ⓑ ⓒ ⓓ		

Chapter 14

Agriculture

MCQs 1 Mark Questions

1. In India, Jhumming, a primitive form of cultivation, is called 'Bewar' or 'Dahiya' in ....
   (a) Odisha
   (b) Chhattisgarh
   (c) Andhra Pradesh
   (d) Madhya Pradesh

2. Which type of agriculture is called 'slash and burn' agriculture?
   (a) Plantation
   (b) Intensive
   (c) Primitive subsistence
   (d) Extensive

3. What does the word 'Olericulture' refer to?
   (a) Cultivation of fruits
   (b) Cultivation of vegetables
   (c) Cultivation of oil seeds
   (d) Cultivation of cash crops

4. Which among the following has the function of recommending Minimum Support Prices for various commodities to the government?
   (a) National Farmers Commission
   (b) Commission for agricultural costs and prices
   (c) Central Statistical Organisation
   (d) Department of Agriculture

5. Which among the following is the largest cotton growing state in India?
   (a) Gujarat (b) Bihar
   (c) Tamil Nadu (d) Karnataka

6. Which of the following are plantation crops?
   (a) Rice and maize
   (b) Wheat and pulses
   (c) Tea, coffee, banana and sugarcane
   (d) None of the above

7. Complete the given analogy.
   Rabi crop : ? : : Kharif crop : Rice
   (a) Soybean
   (b) Millet
   (c) Barley
   (d) Pulses

8. Name the three major cropping seasons for Indian agriculture.
   (a) Aus, Aman and Boro
   (b) Rabi, Kharif and Zaid
   (c) Baisakh, Paus and Chait
   (d) None of the above

9. Which of the following is not a cash crop in India?
(a) Sugarcane (b) Cashew
(c) Tobacco (d) Wheat

10. What is the main food crop of the Eastern and Southern part of the country?
(a) Rice (b) Wheat (c) Maize (d) Sugarcane

11. Which among the following are the two main wheat growing regions of India?
(a) The Ganga-Sutlej Plains and the Deccan Trap
(b) North-Eastern Part and Eastern-Coastal Plains
(c) Deccan Plateau and Konkan Coast
(d) None of the above

12. Which of the following is the third most important food crop of our country?
(a) Rice (b) Wheat
(c) Jowar (d) Bajra

13. Under which plan did the government introduce an agricultural strategy which gave rise to Green Revolution?
(a) First Five Year Plan
(b) Second Five Year Plan
(c) Third Five Year Plan
(d) Fourth Five Year Plan

14. Which of the following crops is a major source of protein in a vegetarian diet?
(a) Wheat (b) Rice
(c) Pulses (d) Oilseeds

15. Which one of the following is not correct for pulses?
(a) Pulses are grown in both rabi and kharif season.
(b) Pulses are leguminous crops.
(c) They are grown in rotation with other crops.
(d) Pulses require intensive irrigation facilities.

16. 'Golden Revolution' is related to ....
(a) precious metals
(b) pulses
(c) jute
(d) horticulture and honey

17. Which of the following conditions can spoil tea crop?
(a) Frequent showers evenly distributed over the year
(b) Frost free climate
(c) Deep fertile well drained soil
(d) Clayey soil which has high water holding capacity

18. Where did coffee cultivation was first introduced?
(a) Himalayas
(b) Aravalli Hills
(c) Garo Hills
(d) Baba Budan Hills

19. Which of the following crops is an important raw material for automobile industry?
(a) Pulses (b) Rice
(c) Rubber (d) None of these

20. Rearing of silk worms for the production of silk fibre is known as ....
(a) sericulture (b) aquaculture
(c) apiculture (d) pisciculture

21. Name the crop which is known as golden fibre.
(a) Cotton (b) Jute
(c) Wool (d) Silk

22. What describes a system of agriculture where a single crop is grown on a large area?
(a) Shifting agriculture
(b) Plantation agriculture
(c) Horticulture
(d) Intensive agriculture

23. Which one of the following is announced by the government in support of a crop?
(a) Maximum support price
(b) Minimum support price
(c) Moderate support price
(d) Influential support price

24. Plantation agriculture is a type of ....
(a) subsistence farming
(b) commercial farming
(c) mixed farming
(d) None of the above

25. Which among the following states is the largest producer of chilli in India?
(a) Madhya Pradesh
(b) West Bengal
(c) Andhra Pradesh
(d) Rajasthan

26. 'Operation Flood' is a ....
(a) mission to increase performance of the dairy sector
(b) river management mission
(c) mission to save rain water for irrigation
(d) mission to increase underground water

27. Which of the following statements is not correct?
(a) India is the second largest producer of fruits in the world.
(b) India is the biggest producer of vegetables in the world.
(c) Production of fruits, vegetables and spices called horticulture.
(d) Uttar Pradesh is the largest producer of the wheat in India.

28. The Green Revolution was successful in parts of Rajasthan, Punjab, Haryana and ....
(a) Western Uttar Pradesh
(b) Eastern Uttar Pradesh
(c) Madhya Pradesh
(d) Gujarat

29. Who is known as the 'Milkman of India'?
(a) M Swaminathan
(b) Verghese Kurien
(c) Dr Arun Krishnan
(d) Vishal Tewari

MCQs 2 Marks Questions

30. There are two statements marked as Assertion (A) and Reason (R). Mark your answer as per the codes given below.
Assertion (A) The Banjaras are a nomadic group which live in the villages of Rajasthan, Punjab, Uttar Pradesh, Madhya Pradesh and Maharashtra.
Reason (R) The Banjaras move with their cattle over long distances in search of pasturelands.
Codes
(a) Both A and R are true and R is the correct explanation of A
(b) Both A and R are true, but R is not the correct explanation of A
(c) A is true, but R is false
(d) A is false, but R is true

31. Read the following statements about various revolutions and select the option that correctly identifies true (T) and false (F) ones.
I. Brown Revolution is related to cocoa.
II. Pink Revolution is related to flowers.
III. Blue Revolution is related to fish production.
IV. Green Revolution is related to environment.
Codes

	I	II	III	IV		I	II	III	IV
(a)	T	T	T	T	(b)	T	F	T	F
(c)	F	T	F	F	(d)	F	F	T	T

32. Consider the following statements and choose the correct option.

I. Green Revolution means increase in production of food grains.

II. It also helped in growth of green plants to maintain ecological balance.

III. Soil erosion was reduced due to this.

Codes

(a) I and III

(b) Only I

(c) II and III

(d) Only III

33. Identify the crop cultivation of India with the help of the information given below.

It is a kharif crop and requires 6 to 8 months to mature. It grows well in drier parts of the black soil of the Deccan Plateau. It requires very light irrigation or rainfall.

(a) Pulses

(b) Cotton

(c) Maize

(d) Sugarcane

34. Identify the type of farming with the help of the information given below.

This type of farming is practiced to meet the needs of the farmer's family. Traditionally, low levels of technology and household labour are used to produce on small output.

(a) Subsistence farming

(b) Shifting cultivation

(c) Commercial farming

(d) Plantations farming

35. Match the following.

List I	List II
A. Kharif crops	1. Wheat, gram
B. Rabi crops	2. Urea and phosphate
C. Chemical fertiliser	3. Animal dung and plant waste
D. Organic manure	4. Paddy, maize

Codes

	A	B	C	D		A	B	C	D
(a)	1	2	3	4	(b)	4	1	2	3
(c)	4	3	2	1	(d)	3	4	1	2

Darken your choice with HB Pencil

1. ⓐ ⓑ ⓒ ⓓ	7. ⓐ ⓑ ⓒ ⓓ	13. ⓐ ⓑ ⓒ ⓓ	19. ⓐ ⓑ ⓒ ⓓ	25. ⓐ ⓑ ⓒ ⓓ	31. ⓐ ⓑ ⓒ ⓓ
2. ⓐ ⓑ ⓒ ⓓ	8. ⓐ ⓑ ⓒ ⓓ	14. ⓐ ⓑ ⓒ ⓓ	20. ⓐ ⓑ ⓒ ⓓ	26. ⓐ ⓑ ⓒ ⓓ	32. ⓐ ⓑ ⓒ ⓓ
3. ⓐ ⓑ ⓒ ⓓ	9. ⓐ ⓑ ⓒ ⓓ	15. ⓐ ⓑ ⓒ ⓓ	21. ⓐ ⓑ ⓒ ⓓ	27. ⓐ ⓑ ⓒ ⓓ	33. ⓐ ⓑ ⓒ ⓓ
4. ⓐ ⓑ ⓒ ⓓ	10. ⓐ ⓑ ⓒ ⓓ	16. ⓐ ⓑ ⓒ ⓓ	22. ⓐ ⓑ ⓒ ⓓ	28. ⓐ ⓑ ⓒ ⓓ	34. ⓐ ⓑ ⓒ ⓓ
5. ⓐ ⓑ ⓒ ⓓ	11. ⓐ ⓑ ⓒ ⓓ	17. ⓐ ⓑ ⓒ ⓓ	23. ⓐ ⓑ ⓒ ⓓ	29. ⓐ ⓑ ⓒ ⓓ	35. ⓐ ⓑ ⓒ ⓓ
6. ⓐ ⓑ ⓒ ⓓ	12. ⓐ ⓑ ⓒ ⓓ	18. ⓐ ⓑ ⓒ ⓓ	24. ⓐ ⓑ ⓒ ⓓ	30. ⓐ ⓑ ⓒ ⓓ	

Chapter 15

Industries

MCQs 1 Mark Questions

1. In which of the following states is Kalpakkam Nuclear Power Plant located?
(a) Tamil Nadu (b) Kerala
(c) Odisha (d) Gujarat

2. Which among the following states has the largest number of cotton textile mills in India?
(a) Gujarat (b) Maharashtra
(c) Madhya Pradesh (d) West Bengal

3. Identify the name of city, which is known as Boston of the East.
(a) Ahmedabad (b) Surat
(c) Mumbai (d) Calcutta

4. Which among the following is a centre of woolen textiles?
(a) Indore (b) Porbandar
(c) Ujjain (d) Bikaner

5. Identify the name of the city, which is known as Manchester of North India.
(a) Kanpur (b) Delhi
(c) Agra (d) Lucknow

6. Which of the following is a centre of cotton textiles?
(a) Jalgaon (b) Kolar
(c) Jaipur (d) Ludhiana

7. Which industries are also known as village or household industries?
(a) Small scale industries
(b) Cottage industries
(c) Large scale industries
(d) Forest based industries

8. Identify the industry use bauxite as a raw material.
(a) Aluminium (b) Cement
(c) Jute (d) Steel

9. The first successful textile mill was established in ………… in 1854.
(a) Bombay (b) Calcutta
(c) Surat (d) Madras

10. The Bhilai Steel Plant was constructed with the collaboration of which country?
(a) Germany (b) Russia
(c) England (d) USA

11. Which one of the following is a major shipbuilding centre of India?
(a) Kandla (b) Paradip
(c) Cochin (d) Tuticorin

12. Basket weaving falls in the category of………… .
(a) small scale industry
(b) cottage industry
(c) large scale industry
(d) None of the above

13. Which one of the following is presently the largest oil refinery of India?
(a) Visakhapatnam (HPCL)
(b) Mathura (IOC)
(c) Vadodara (IOC)
(d) Mumbai (BPCL)

14. Indian Institute of Sugarcane Research is located at ....
(a) Lucknow (b) Coimbatore
(c) Mumbai (d) Surat

15. Which one of the following places with petrochemical industries is most Westward located in India?
(a) Barauni (b) Nagpur
(c) Kota (d) Ujjain

16. Identify the incorrectly matched pair.
(a) Public Sector – BHEL
(b) Electric Power Generation – NTPC
(c) Private Sector – SAIL
(d) Joint Sector – OIL

17. In India, maximum number of workers are employed in ....
(a) textile industry
(b) automobile industry
(c) iron and steel industry
(d) tea industry

18. NALCO and BALCO are associated with which of the following?
(a) Aluminium industry
(b) Cement industry
(c) Fertiliser industry
(d) Paper industry

19. Which of the following states ranks first in terms of the maximum number of agro-based industries?
(a) West Bengal (b) Gujarat
(c) Punjab (d) Assam

MCQs 2 Marks Questions

20. Identify the industry of India with the help of the information given below.
- This industry is mainly based on non-metallic minerals.
- Its major raw materials are limestone and coal.

(a) Iron and steel industry
(b) Cement industry
(c) Petrochemical industry
(d) Fertiliser industry

21. Match the following.

List I (Cottage Industrial Products)	**List II** (Producing Centres)
A. Silk Saree	1. Moradabad
B. Chicken Kurti	2. Gorakhpur
C. Terracotta	3. Varanasi
D. Brass	4. Lucknow

Codes

	A	B	C	D		A	B	C	D
(a)	4	3	1	2	(b)	3	4	2	1
(c)	1	2	3	4	(d)	2	1	4	3

22. Consider the following statements regarding the major challenges faced by the sugar industry in India and choose the correct option.
I. Seasonal nature of the industry.
II. Old and inefficient method of production.
III. Transport delay in reaching to sugar factories.

Codes
(a) Only I
(b) Only II
(c) Both II and III
(d) All of the above

23. There are two statements marked as Assertion (A) and Reason (R). Mark your answer as per the codes given below.

Assertion (A) India is the largest producer of raw jute and jute goods.

Reason (R) The small and marginal farmers are engaged in the production of jute.

Codes

(a) Both A and R are true and R is the correct explanation of A
(b) Both A and R are true, but R is not the correct explanation of A
(c) A is true, but R is false
(d) A is false, but R is true

24. Consider the following statements regarding industries of India and select the option that correctly identifies true (T) and false (F) ones.

I. Aluminium smelting is the second most important metallurgical industry in India.
II. India stands second in the world in sugar production.
III. Raw materials used in manufacturing of cement are limestone, silica, alumina and gypsum.
IV. Mineral industry is used for manufacturing aircrafts, utensils and wires.

Codes

	I	II	III	IV		I	II	III	IV
(a)	T	T	T	T	(b)	F	T	T	F
(c)	T	T	F	F	(d)	F	F	T	T

25. Identify the industries of India marked as A and B on the map given below.

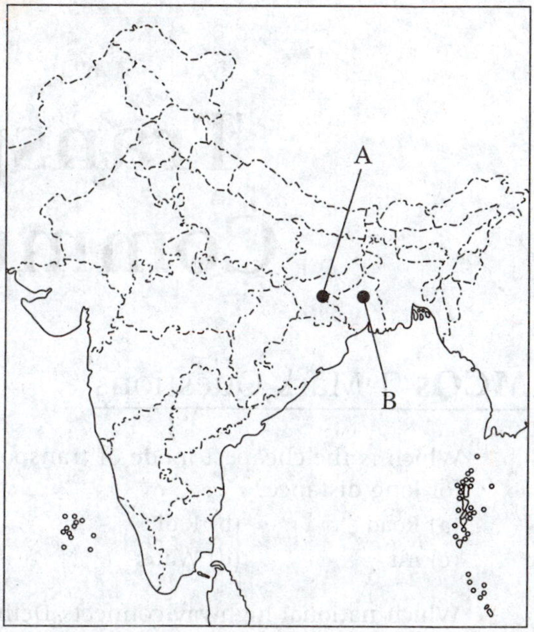

Codes

	A	B
(a)	Rourkela Steel Plant	Durgapur Steel Plant
(b)	Durgapur Steel Plant	Bokaro Steel Plant
(c)	Jamshedpur Iron and Steel Plant	Durgapur Steel Plant
(d)	Tata Iron and Steel Plant	Coimbatore Steel Plant

Darken your choice with HB Pencil

1. ⓐ ⓑ ⓒ ⓓ	6. ⓐ ⓑ ⓒ ⓓ	11. ⓐ ⓑ ⓒ ⓓ	16. ⓐ ⓑ ⓒ ⓓ	21. ⓐ ⓑ ⓒ ⓓ
2. ⓐ ⓑ ⓒ ⓓ	7. ⓐ ⓑ ⓒ ⓓ	12. ⓐ ⓑ ⓒ ⓓ	17. ⓐ ⓑ ⓒ ⓓ	22. ⓐ ⓑ ⓒ ⓓ
3. ⓐ ⓑ ⓒ ⓓ	8. ⓐ ⓑ ⓒ ⓓ	13. ⓐ ⓑ ⓒ ⓓ	18. ⓐ ⓑ ⓒ ⓓ	23. ⓐ ⓑ ⓒ ⓓ
4. ⓐ ⓑ ⓒ ⓓ	9. ⓐ ⓑ ⓒ ⓓ	14. ⓐ ⓑ ⓒ ⓓ	19. ⓐ ⓑ ⓒ ⓓ	24. ⓐ ⓑ ⓒ ⓓ
5. ⓐ ⓑ ⓒ ⓓ	10. ⓐ ⓑ ⓒ ⓓ	15. ⓐ ⓑ ⓒ ⓓ	20. ⓐ ⓑ ⓒ ⓓ	25. ⓐ ⓑ ⓒ ⓓ

Chapter 16

Transport and Communication

MCQs 1 Mark Questions

1. Which is the cheapest mode of transport for long distance?
(a) Road (b) Rail
(c) Air (d) Water

2. Which national highway connects Delhi and Kolkata via Varanasi?
(a) NH-4 (b) NH-10
(c) NH-2 (d) NH-6

3. Where is the headquarters of South-Central Railway located?
(a) Bilaspur (b) Mumbai
(c) Secunderabad (d) Jabalpur

4. Golden Quadrilateral Project for the development of National Highways was initiated by ....
(a) PV Narasimha Rao
(b) IK Gujral
(c) Manmohan Singh
(d) Atal Bihari Vajpayee

5. Which one of the following national highways passes through Maharashtra, Chhattisgarh and Odisha?
(a) NH-4 (b) NH-5
(c) NH-6 (d) NH-7

6. Which ports are located on the Eastern coast of India?
(a) Kandla and Haldia
(b) Haldia and Kochin
(c) Paradip and Kandla
(d) Paradip and Haldia

7. Which is the longest national highway in India?
(a) NH-4 (b) NH-44
(c) NH-10 (d) NH-5

8. The National Highway-1D connects Leh to Kashmir Valley through the .... pass.
(a) Khyber (b) Zojila
(c) Nathula (d) Karakoram

9. Which one of the following is a correct sequence of the Indian ports from North to South?
(a) Haldia, Kandla, Paradip, Kochi
(b) Kandla, Haldia, Paradip, Kochi
(c) Kandla, Haldia, Kochi, Paradip
(d) Kochi, Kandla, Haldia, Paradip

10. Identify the name of ports, which is known as 'Diamond Harbour'.
(a) Haldia Port (b) Paradip Port
(c) Cochin Port (d) Kandla Port

11. Which of the following is the longest side of the Golden Quadrilateral?

(a) Delhi-Mumbai (b) Mumbai-Chennai
(c) Chennai-Kolkata (d) Kolkata-Delhi

12. Identify the incorrectly matched pair.

	Railway	Zone Headquarters
(a)	North-Eastern Railway	– Gorakhpur
(b)	South-Eastern Railway	– Bhubaneswar
(c)	Eastern-Railway	– Kolkata
(d)	South-East Central Railway	– Bilaspur

13. Which of the following is the deepest landlocked protected port of India?

(a) Haldia (b) Jawaharlal Nehru
(c) Chennai (d) Visakhapatnam

14. Which among the following is the tidal port?

(a) Visakhapatnam Port
(b) Tuticorin Port
(c) Kandla Port
(d) Paradip Port

15. When was the first artificial satellite for communication launched?

(a) 1981 (b) 1991
(c) 1957 (d) 1954

16. Which of the following methods is used to communicate quickly with one or many individuals in various locations?

(a) Face to Face (b) E-mail
(c) Notices/Posters (d) Business Meetings

MCQs 2 Mark Questions

17. Consider the following statements with reference to National Highways Development Project (NHDP) and choose the correct option.

I. Belgaum and Nellore lie on the Golden Quadrilateral.

II. Vadodara and Jhansi lie on the East–West Corridor.

III. Ambala and Kanpur lie on the North–South Corridor.

Codes

(a) I, II and III (b) II and III
(c) I and II (d) Only I

18. Match the following.

List I (Railway Zone)	List II (Headquarters Centres)
A. Northern	1. Allahabad
B. North-Western	2. New Delhi
C. North-Centre	3. Jaipur

Codes

	A	B	C		A	B	C
(a)	2	3	1	(b)	3	1	2
(c)	1	2	3	(d)	3	2	1

19. Consider the following statements with reference to Indian transport systems and choose the correct option.

I. Indian railways routes are divided into three parts namely meter gauge, broad gauge, and narrow gauge.

II. The Northern plain of India has higher East-West railway connectivity than the North-South railway connectivity.

Codes

(a) Only I (b) Only II
(c) Both I and II (d) Neither I nor II

20 Identify the biggest port of India with the help of information given below.

- It is a natural deep-water habour port which lies on the West coast of India. This port has played a significant role in Industrial Development of India and it is mainly imports liquid chemicals, petroleum products and mineral oil, etc.

(a) Mumbai Port (b) Tuticorin Port
(c) Kandla Port (d) Visakhapatnam

21. There are two statements marked as Assertion (A) and Reason (R). Mark your answer as per the codes given below.

Assertion (A) Airways transport is the best option to provide relief material in the disaster affected areas.

Reason (R) Airways transport are one of the most comfortable and fastest modes of transportation.

Codes

(a) Both A and R are true and R is the correct explanation of A
(b) Both A and R are true, but R is not the correct explanation of A
(c) A is true, but R is false
(d) A is false, but R is true

22. Read the given statements and select the option that correctly identifies true (T) and false (F) ones.

I. Satellite communication can be used to send messages to inaccessible areas.
II. In an organisation, e-mail is the most common means of written communication.

Code

	I	II		I	II
(a)	T	T	(b)	F	T
(c)	T	F	(d)	F	F

23. Identify the railway zones and their head quarters marked as A and B on the map given below.

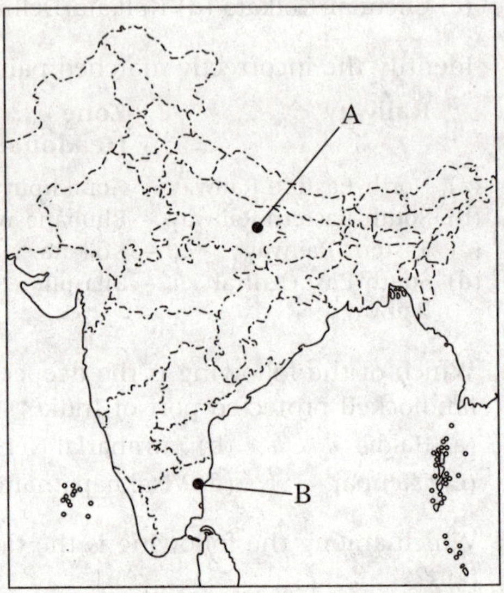

	A	B
(a)	North-Eastern – Gorakhpur	Southern – Chennai
(b)	Northern – Lucknow	South-Eastern – Bilaspur
(c)	North-Eastern – Gorakhpur	South-Eastern – Bilaspur
(d)	Northern – Lucknow	Southern – Chennai

Darken your choice with HB Pencil

1. ⓐ ⓑ ⓒ ⓓ	5. ⓐ ⓑ ⓒ ⓓ	9. ⓐ ⓑ ⓒ ⓓ	13. ⓐ ⓑ ⓒ ⓓ	17. ⓐ ⓑ ⓒ ⓓ	21. ⓐ ⓑ ⓒ ⓓ
2. ⓐ ⓑ ⓒ ⓓ	6. ⓐ ⓑ ⓒ ⓓ	10. ⓐ ⓑ ⓒ ⓓ	14. ⓐ ⓑ ⓒ ⓓ	18. ⓐ ⓑ ⓒ ⓓ	22. ⓐ ⓑ ⓒ ⓓ
3. ⓐ ⓑ ⓒ ⓓ	7. ⓐ ⓑ ⓒ ⓓ	11. ⓐ ⓑ ⓒ ⓓ	15. ⓐ ⓑ ⓒ ⓓ	19. ⓐ ⓑ ⓒ ⓓ	23. ⓐ ⓑ ⓒ ⓓ
4. ⓐ ⓑ ⓒ ⓓ	8. ⓐ ⓑ ⓒ ⓓ	12. ⓐ ⓑ ⓒ ⓓ	16. ⓐ ⓑ ⓒ ⓓ	20. ⓐ ⓑ ⓒ ⓓ	

Chapter 17

Human Resources

MCQs 1 Mark Questions

1. According to the census 2011, which among the following is the most populous state of India?
(a) Maharashtra
(b) Rajasthan
(c) Bihar
(d) Uttar Pradesh

2. What is the annual number of live births per 1,000 people called?
(a) General fertility rate
(b) Crude birth rate
(c) Total fertility rate
(d) Gross reproduction rate

3. From which of the following do we get information about the population of a country?
(a) Census
(b) By counting the people
(c) Both (a) and (b)
(d) By dividing

4. In which year, the first complete census was held?
(a) 1876 (b) 1881
(c) 1889 (d) 1891

5. A high growth rate of population is characterised by ....
(a) high birth and high death rates
(b) high birth and low death rates
(c) low birth and low death rates
(d) low birth and high death rates

6. In India, population density is defined as the number of persons ....
(a) per square mile
(b) per lakh square mile
(c) per lakh square kilometer
(d) per square kilometer

7. Which of the following plays a very significant role in changing the composition and distribution of population?
(a) Death rates
(b) Birth rates
(c) Migration
(d) All of the above

8. What do you mean by census?
(a) Total number of babies born
(b) Official counting of population done after every ten years
(c) Total number of infants that are vaccinated
(d) Recording of births and deaths every year

9. Complete the given analogy.
Birth rate : Death rate : : Immigration : ?
(a) Mortality (b) Migration
(c) Emigration (d) Growth rate

10. As per the census 2011, which among the following has the highest population density?
(a) Nagaland
(b) Bihar
(c) Maharashtra
(d) Uttar Pradesh

11. What is an important indicator of population composition that represents the number of people of different age groups?
(a) Density of population
(b) Age structure
(c) Sex ratio
(d) Physiological density

12. The Government of India has a Ministry of Human Resource Development. The ministry was created in the year ....
(a) 1993 (b) 1985
(c) 1980 (d) 1998

13. Which one of the following is the most labour intensive sector in India?
(a) Agriculture
(b) Fisheries
(c) Poultry Farming
(d) Mining

14. Which one of the following is the main reason for male migration in India?
(a) Education
(b) Business
(c) Work and Employment
(d) Marriage

15. What is considered as superior to other resources such as land, physical capital, etc?
(a) Education
(b) Resource management
(c) Industrialisation
(d) Human capital

16. Which of the following is the social consequence of migration?
(a) Intermixing of people from diverse cultures
(b) Change in sex ratio
(c) Women empowerment
(d) Remittances

17. Identify the type of unemployment which is/are common in rural areas.
(a) Seasonal unemployment
(b) Disguised unemployment
(c) Both (a) and (b)
(d) Unseasonal unemployment

18. What is the major reason for female migration in India?
(a) Business (b) Marriage
(c) Work (d) Education

19. Which one of the following streams are dominated by male migrants in India?
(a) Rural-urban (b) Urban-urban
(c) Rural-rural (d) Urban-rural

MCQs 2 Marks Questions

20. Consider the following statements and choose the correct option.
I. Migration is an important determinant of population change.
II. Immigration is a process through which individuals become permanent residents or citizens of another country.

Codes
(a) Only I (b) Only II
(c) Both I and II (d) Neither I nor II

21. Which among the following is/are the components of population change?
I. Birth II. Death
III. Skills IV. Migration

Codes
(a) Only I (b) I and II
(c) I, II and IV (d) All of these

22. Consider the following statements and choose the correct option.

I. Birth rate is the number of live births per 1000 persons in a year.

II. The Maternal Mortality Rate (MMR) is the number of maternal death per 1,00,000 live births in a given year.

Codes

(a) Only I (b) Only II

(c) Both I and II (d) Neither I nor II

23. Match the following.

List I (Subjects)		**List II** (Meaning)
A. Immigration	1.	Coming of people into a country
B. Demographic	2.	Better health services
C. Push factor	3.	Leaving one's own country
D. Pull factor	4.	Insurgency

Codes

	A	B	C	D
(a)	1	2	3	4
(b)	4	3	2	1
(c)	2	3	4	1
(d)	1	4	2	3

24. Arrange the following reasons of female migration by last residence in descending order as per their percentage.

I. Work

II. Education

III. Moved after birth

IV. Business

Codes

(a) I, II, III, IV (b) IV, II, III, I

(c) III, II, IV, I (d) III, II, I, IV

25. Identify the scheme programme with the help of the information given below.

- It is a flagship programme of the government of India that was started in 2001 to achieve the universalisation of elementary education.
- The main aim of the programme is to provide elementary education of all children in the age group of 6 to 14 years.

(a) Sarva Shiksha Abhiyan

(b) Mid day Meal Scheme

(c) Integrated Child Development Scheme

(d) None of the above

26. Match the following.

List I		**List II**
A. Infant Mortality	1.	Number of females per 1000 males
B. Sex Ratio	2.	Number of live birth for every 1000 people in a year
C. Birth Rate	3.	Number of deaths of infants per 1000 of births in a year
D. Life Expectancy	4.	Average length of life that a new born is expected to live

Codes

	A	B	C	D
(a)	1	2	3	4
(b)	4	3	2	1
(c)	2	4	1	3
(d)	3	1	2	4

Darken your choice with HB Pencil

1. ⓐ ⓑ ⓒ ⓓ	6. ⓐ ⓑ ⓒ ⓓ	11. ⓐ ⓑ ⓒ ⓓ	16. ⓐ ⓑ ⓒ ⓓ	21. ⓐ ⓑ ⓒ ⓓ	26. ⓐ ⓑ ⓒ ⓓ
2. ⓐ ⓑ ⓒ ⓓ	7. ⓐ ⓑ ⓒ ⓓ	12. ⓐ ⓑ ⓒ ⓓ	17. ⓐ ⓑ ⓒ ⓓ	22. ⓐ ⓑ ⓒ ⓓ	
3. ⓐ ⓑ ⓒ ⓓ	8. ⓐ ⓑ ⓒ ⓓ	13. ⓐ ⓑ ⓒ ⓓ	18. ⓐ ⓑ ⓒ ⓓ	23. ⓐ ⓑ ⓒ ⓓ	
4. ⓐ ⓑ ⓒ ⓓ	9. ⓐ ⓑ ⓒ ⓓ	14. ⓐ ⓑ ⓒ ⓓ	19. ⓐ ⓑ ⓒ ⓓ	24. ⓐ ⓑ ⓒ ⓓ	
5. ⓐ ⓑ ⓒ ⓓ	10. ⓐ ⓑ ⓒ ⓓ	15. ⓐ ⓑ ⓒ ⓓ	20. ⓐ ⓑ ⓒ ⓓ	25. ⓐ ⓑ ⓒ ⓓ	

Chapter 18

Money and Banking

MCQs 1 Mark Questions

1. A system where goods were exchanged without using money is better known as ....
   (a) goods system (b) exchange system
   (c) no-money system (d) barter system

2. Which of the following is a source of informal sector of loan?
   (a) Moneylenders (b) Cooperative Bank
   (c) Central Bank (d) Commercial Bank

3. Which among the following is/are a form of collateral type of security taken by the banks from its customers?
   (a) Vehicle
   (b) Property
   (c) Both (a) and (b)
   (d) Saving Account

4. Which one of the following was one of the objectives of demonetisation in 2016?
   (a) To gift new notes to people of India
   (b) To reduce and prevent circulation of black money in the market
   (c) To increase the interest rate
   (d) To increase the value of currency

5. Online and mobile banking is an example of ....
   (a) unit banking
   (b) shadow banking
   (c) universal banking
   (d) direct banking

6. Which agency regulates the money supply in India?
   (a) The Government of India
   (b) Commercial Banks
   (c) Reserve Bank of India
   (d) None of the above

7. Which one is included in the primary function of money?
   (a) Medium of exchange
   (b) Measure of value
   (c) Both (a) and (b)
   (d) Store of value

8. Who undertakes the distribution of one rupee notes and coins and small coins all over the country?
   (a) Finance Ministry
   (b) RBI
   (c) Home Ministry
   (d) All of the above

9. A 'debt trap' in money and banking means ....
(a) inability to repay credit amount
(b) ability to pay credit amount
(c) overspending till no money is left
(d) None of the above

10. Which of the following banks is authorised to act as an agent of RBI?
(a) State Bank of India
(b) Punjab National Bank
(c) ICICI Bank
(d) HDFC Bank

11. Which among the following statements is incorrect?
(a) RBI is the bank of issue.
(b) RBI acts as banker to the government.
(c) RBI is banker's bank.
(d) RBI does not regulate the flow of credit.

12. The Reserve Bank of India was established on ....
(a) 1st April, 1935 (b) 12th July, 1982
(c) 26th May, 2006 (d) 30th September, 2005

13. Which movement encouraged the formation of commercial banks?
(a) Swadeshi Movement
(b) Quit India Movement
(c) Non-Cooperation Movement
(d) Civil Disobedience Movement

14. Which is the largest commercial bank of the country?
(a) Bank of India
(b) Canara Bank
(c) State Bank of India
(d) Union Bank of India

15. Complete the given analogy.
Private owned : HDFC : : Central Bank : ?
(a) Reserve Bank of India
(b) State Bank of India
(c) Punjab National Bank
(d) Union Bank

16. Which of the following is the plastic money?
(a) Debit card
(b) Credit card
(c) Both (a) and (b)
(d) Demand deposits

17. People also have the provision to withdraw the money as and when the require the deposits in the bank accounts to be withdrawn, what are these deposits called?
(a) Fixed deposits (b) Savings
(c) Demand deposits (d) Demand drafts

18. Which is one of the major reason which prevent the poor from getting bank loans?
(a) Illiteracy
(b) Lack of availability of banks in rural areas
(c) Absence of collateral
(d) Shy to approach formal organisations

19. Which of the following is not the function of the Reserve Bank of India?
(a) Acting as a Banker to the Government
(b) Keeping of Foreign Exchange Reserve
(c) Issuing of Coins
(d) Regulating Credit in the Country

20. Select the correct order of money evolution.
(a) Commodity Money, Paper Money, Metal Money
(b) Commodity Money, Metal Money, Paper Money
(c) Metal Money, Paper Money, Commodity Money
(d) None of the above

MCQs 2 Marks Questions

21. Identify the system of payment with the help of the information given below.
    - It is an act of trading goods or services between two or more parties without the use of money.
    - It is an old method of exchange. People exchanged services and goods for other services and goods in return.

    (a) Goods system
    (b) Exchange system
    (c) No-money system
    (d) Barter system

22. There are two statements marked as Assertion (A) and Reason (R). Mark your answer as per the codes given below.

    Assertion (A) RBI gives licence to commercial banks and supervises them.
    Reason (R) RBI is the largest bank of the country.

    Codes
    (a) Both A and R are true and R is the correct explanation of A
    (b) Both A and R are true, but R is not the correct explanation of A
    (c) A is true, but R is false
    (d) A is false, but R is true

23. Read the given statements and select the option that correctly identifies true (T) and false (F) ones.

    I. A bank is a financial institution that allows people to make deposits and receive credit.
    II. Banking is an industry that allows credit, handless deposits, and provides financial help to borrowers.
    III. Banking has become an integral part, as it facilitates advancing loans to different entities.

    Codes

	I	II	III
(a)	T	T	T
(b)	F	T	T
(c)	T	T	F
(d)	F	F	T

24. Consider the following statements and choose the correct option.

    I. Money is recognised as a means for purchasing goods and services and repayment of debts.
    II. It has become an essential means of exchange in the entire world.

    Codes
    (a) Only I (b) Only II
    (c) Both I and II (d) Neither I nor II

Darken your choice with HB Pencil

1. ⓐ ⓑ ⓒ ⓓ	5. ⓐ ⓑ ⓒ ⓓ	9. ⓐ ⓑ ⓒ ⓓ	13. ⓐ ⓑ ⓒ ⓓ	17. ⓐ ⓑ ⓒ ⓓ	21. ⓐ ⓑ ⓒ ⓓ
2. ⓐ ⓑ ⓒ ⓓ	6. ⓐ ⓑ ⓒ ⓓ	10. ⓐ ⓑ ⓒ ⓓ	14. ⓐ ⓑ ⓒ ⓓ	18. ⓐ ⓑ ⓒ ⓓ	22. ⓐ ⓑ ⓒ ⓓ
3. ⓐ ⓑ ⓒ ⓓ	7. ⓐ ⓑ ⓒ ⓓ	11. ⓐ ⓑ ⓒ ⓓ	15. ⓐ ⓑ ⓒ ⓓ	19. ⓐ ⓑ ⓒ ⓓ	23. ⓐ ⓑ ⓒ ⓓ
4. ⓐ ⓑ ⓒ ⓓ	8. ⓐ ⓑ ⓒ ⓓ	12. ⓐ ⓑ ⓒ ⓓ	16. ⓐ ⓑ ⓒ ⓓ	20. ⓐ ⓑ ⓒ ⓓ	24. ⓐ ⓑ ⓒ ⓓ

Chapter

19

Constitution and Its Features

MCQs 1 Mark Questions

1. In which year, was the Constitution of India adopted by the Constituent Assembly?
(a) 1948 (b) 1956
(c) 1949 (d) 1950

2. Mahatma Gandhi' vision about the Indian Constitution was published in which of the following magazines?
(a) Young India
(b) Discovery of India
(c) New India
(d) India Gazette

3. Who is considered as the 'Father of the Constitution of India'?
(a) Dr BR Ambedkar
(b) Dr Rajendra Prasad
(c) Jawaharlal Nehru
(d) MN Roy

4. Identify the name of personality who became the Vice-Chairman of the Constituent Assembly as shown in the image given below.

(a) Sardar Patel
(b) Jaipal Singh
(c) HC Mookherjee
(d) Baldev Singh

5. Which of the following countries' Constitution was not referred to while making the Indian Constitution?
(a) United Kingdom
(b) USA
(c) France
(d) Italy

6. Which one of the following is not a part of the Preamble of the Indian Constitution?
(a) Socialism (b) Federalism
(c) Secularism (d) Democratic

7. The Constitution of India borrowed the Rule of Law and Parliamentary Government from which country's Constitution?
(a) France
(b) United Kingdom
(c) United States of America
(d) None of the above

8. How much time did the Constituent Assembly take to file the final draft of the Constitution of India?
(a) 2 years, 1 month, 11 days
(b) 2 years, 11 months, 18 days
(c) 1 year, 11 months, 15 days
(d) 2 years, 10 months, 16 days

9. Identify the name of personality, who became the temporary President of the Constituent Assembly.
(a) Dr Sachchidananda Sinha
(b) Rajendra Prasad
(c) Sardar Vallabhbhai Patel
(d) Jawaharlal Nehru

10. Which of the following is not considered one of the Fundamental Rights according to the Constitution of India?
(a) Right to Freedom
(b) Right to Constitutional Remedies
(c) Right to Equality
(d) Right to Property

11. Which article has contributed to eradicating untouchability from the Constitution of India?
(a) Article 18 (b) Article 12
(c) Article 17 (d) Article 11

12. Who has the authority to remove the Vice-President of India from their power?
(a) Prime Minister
(b) Parliament
(c) President
(d) Supreme Court

13. What does Part-IV of the Indian Constitution deal with?
(a) Citizenship
(b) Directive Principles of State Policy
(c) Union Executive
(d) Rights

14. Who is considered as the source of authority according to the Constitution of India?
(a) The Prime Minister
(b) The Bureaucrats
(c) The people of the country India
(d) The Supreme Court

15. By which Constitutional Amendment the words socialist, secular and integrity were incorporated in the Preamble of the Constitution of India?
(a) 4th Amendment
(b) 20th Amendment
(c) 42nd Amendment
(d) 44th Amendment

16. Which of the following options is not considered to be a characteristic of the Indian Constitution?
(a) Democratic system
(b) Single citizenship
(c) Independent Judiciary
(d) Employment gurantee of every citizen

17. What is the name of our country according to our Constitution?
(a) Bharat
(b) Hindustan
(c) Bharatvarsha
(d) Bharat Desha

18. Who presented the first ever Union Budget of India after independence?
(a) RK Shanmukham Chetty
(b) Jawaharlal Nehru
(c) Indira Gandhi
(d) Morarji Ranchhodji Desai

19. Habeas corpus is linked with which part of the Constitution of India?
(a) Fundamental Duties (b) State Policies
(c) Fundamental Rights (d) Preamble

20. The feature of federalism has been adopted in Indian Constitution from which country?
(a) Germany (b) Canada
(c) Italy (d) France

21. Which part of the Indian Constitution is known as the soul of the Constitution?
(a) Fundamental Duties (b) Preamble
(c) Article 32 (d) None of these

MCQs 2 Marks Questions

22. Match of the following.

List I (Countries)	List II (Borrowed Features of Indian Constitution)
A. British Constitution	1. Ideals of liberty, equality and fraternity
B. Canada Constitution	2. Cabinet System
C. USA Constitution	3. Residuary Power
D. French Constitution	4. Independent Judiciary

Codes

	A	B	C	D		A	B	C	D
(a)	3	2	4	1	(b)	2	3	4	1
(c)	2	3	1	4	(d)	3	2	1	4

23. Consider the following statements regarding the official language and choose the correct option.
I. Article 345 of the Indian Constitution deals with the official language or languages of a state.
II. Article 343 of the Indian Constitution deals with the official language of the Union.

Codes
(a) Only I
(b) Only II
(c) Both I and II
(d) Neither I nor II

24. Match the following.

List I (Keyword)	List II (Meaning)
A. Sovereign	1. People have the supreme right to make decisions
B. Republic	2. Head of the state is an elected person
C. Fraternity	3. People should live like brothers and sister
D. Secular	4. The government will not favour any religion

Codes

	A	B	C	D
(a)	1	2	3	4
(b)	2	1	3	4
(c)	3	2	1	4
(d)	1	3	2	4

25. There are two statements marked as Assertion (A) and Reason (R). Mark your answer as per the codes given below.
Assertion (A) The Constitution of a country is a set of written rules that are accepted by all the people living in a country.
Reason (R) It generates a degree of trust and coordination among people that is necessary for different kinds of people living together.

Codes
(a) Both A and R are true and R is the correct explanation of A
(b) Both A and R are true, but R is not the correct explanation of A
(c) A is true, but R is false
(d) A is false, but R is true

26. Consider the following statements regarding Constituent Assembly and choose the correct option.

I. The member of the Constituent Assembly could not have been chosen directly by or the people of India.

II. The Constituent Assembly of India was a sovereign body, which was formed on the recommendation of the Cabinet Mission.

Codes

(a) Only I

(b) Only II

(c) Both I and II

(d) Neither I nor II

27. Consider the following statements and choose the correct option.

I. The urban local bodies were constitutionalised through the 74th Constitutional Amendment Act of 1992.

II. The Constitution provides for the reservation of seats for the Scheduled Castes and the Scheduled Tribes in every municipality in the proportion of their population.

Codes

(a) Only I

(b) Only II

(c) Both I and II

(d) Neither I nor II

Darken your choice with HB Pencil

1. ⓐ ⓑ ⓒ ⓓ	6. ⓐ ⓑ ⓒ ⓓ	11. ⓐ ⓑ ⓒ ⓓ	16. ⓐ ⓑ ⓒ ⓓ	21. ⓐ ⓑ ⓒ ⓓ	26. ⓐ ⓑ ⓒ ⓓ
2. ⓐ ⓑ ⓒ ⓓ	7. ⓐ ⓑ ⓒ ⓓ	12. ⓐ ⓑ ⓒ ⓓ	17. ⓐ ⓑ ⓒ ⓓ	22. ⓐ ⓑ ⓒ ⓓ	27. ⓐ ⓑ ⓒ ⓓ
3. ⓐ ⓑ ⓒ ⓓ	8. ⓐ ⓑ ⓒ ⓓ	13. ⓐ ⓑ ⓒ ⓓ	18. ⓐ ⓑ ⓒ ⓓ	23. ⓐ ⓑ ⓒ ⓓ	
4. ⓐ ⓑ ⓒ ⓓ	9. ⓐ ⓑ ⓒ ⓓ	14. ⓐ ⓑ ⓒ ⓓ	19. ⓐ ⓑ ⓒ ⓓ	24. ⓐ ⓑ ⓒ ⓓ	
5. ⓐ ⓑ ⓒ ⓓ	10. ⓐ ⓑ ⓒ ⓓ	15. ⓐ ⓑ ⓒ ⓓ	20. ⓐ ⓑ ⓒ ⓓ	25. ⓐ ⓑ ⓒ ⓓ	

Chapter 20

Fundamental Rights and DPSPs

MCQs 1 Mark Questions

1. Which part of the Indian Constitution deals with Fundamental Right?
   (a) Part IV (b) Part IV-A
   (c) Part III (d) Part II

2. Which among the following committees gave the justiciable and non-justiciable types of rights?
   (a) Bhure Lal Committee
   (b) Balwant Rai Mehta Committee
   (c) Sapru Committee
   (d) None of the above

3. Which of the following articles of the Indian Constitution contains the Right to Religious Freedom?
   (a) Article 26-29 (b) Article 24-30
   (c) Article 25-28 (d) Article 30-33

4. Article ……… of the Indian Constitution abolishes the practice of untouchability.
   (a) Article 17 (b) Article 16
   (c) Article 18 (d) Article 14

5. Which of the following Fundamental Rights is called as the heart and soul of the Indian Constitution?
   (a) Right to Freedom
   (b) Right to Freedom of Religion
   (c) Right to Constitutional Remedies
   (d) Cultural and Educational Rights

6. Article 21A of the Constitution provides the Right to …………
   (a) Privacy (b) Education
   (c) Equality (d) Justice

7. Which of the following category of the Fundamental Rights in the Indian Constitution includes abolition of untouchability?
   (a) Right to Freedom
   (b) Right to Freedom of Religion
   (c) Right against Exploitation
   (d) Right to Equality

8. Which of the following statements is/are the correct explanation of the Right to Constitutional Remedies?
   (a) It contains the remedies with respect to any Fundamental Right violation.
   (b) It provides solutions to an individuals issues.
   (c) It provides a list of lawyers that could provide any lawyering services for any legal action against an individual.
   (d) All of the above

9. Who among the following is the guardian of Fundamental Rights?
(a) Executive (b) Legislature
(c) Judiciary (d) Political parties

10. Which of the following Fundamental Rights is not given by the Constitution of India?
(a) Right against Exploitation
(b) Right to Freedom
(c) Right to Work
(d) None of the above

11. The Fundamental Rights are given under which of the following articles of the Constitution of India?
(a) Article 12 to 35 (b) Article 11 to 23
(c) Article 110 to 124 (d) None of these

12. Which of the following is correct with respect to 'Right against Exploitation'?
(a) Prohibition of traffic in human beings and forced labour.
(b) Freedom as to payment of taxes for the promotion of any particular region.
(c) Protection of interests of minorities.
(d) Equality below the law.

13. What are the ideals that need to be kept in mind while framing policies called?
(a) Socialism (b) Democracy
(c) Directives Principles of State Policy
(d) Preamble

14. Which among the given articles of the DPSP provides equal pay for both men and women?
(a) Article 38 (b) Article 39
(c) Article 37 (d) Article 38A

15. The concept of welfare state is included in which part of the Indian Constitution?
(a) Fundamental Right
(b) Fundamental Duties
(c) Preamble
(d) Directive Principles of State Policy

16. Protection of monuments and places, and objects of national importance are covered under which of the following parts?
(a) Fundamental Duties
(b) Fundamental Rights
(c) Directive Principles of State Policy
(d) None of the above

17. Identify the name of the famous personality who describes the Directive Principles of State Policy as a novel feature of the Constitution of India.
(a) DD Basu
(b) BR Ambedkar
(c) Jawaharlal Nehru
(d) Mahatma Gandhi

18. Complete the given analogy.
Fundamental Rights (FRs) : USA : : Directive Principles of State Policy (DPSP) : ?
(a) Canada (b) Ireland
(c) United Kingdom (d) France

19. Which part of the Indian Constitution contains the Directive Principles of State Policy?
(a) Part-II (b) Part-I
(c) Part-IV A (d) Part-IV

20. Which part of the Constitution is called the 'Magna Carta' of India?
(a) Part III (b) Part II
(c) Part IV (d) Part IV-A

MCQs 2 Marks Questions

21. Consider the following statements and choose the correct option.
I. The Government of India 1935, became the immediate source of Directive Principle of State Policy (DPSP).
II. DPSP aren't enforceable legally.

Codes

(a) Only I (b) Only II
(c) Both I and II (d) None of these

22. Match the following.

List I (Fundamental Right)	List II (Article)
A. Right to Equality	1. Article (14-18)
B. Right to Freedom	2. Article (19-22)
C. Right against Exploitation	3. Article (23-24)

Codes

	A	B	C		A	B	C
(a)	1	2	3	(b)	1	3	2
(c)	3	1	2	(d)	2	3	1

23. Which of the following are Directive Principles of State Policy of the Constitution of India?

I. Uniform Civil Code
II. Equal pay for equal work
III. Small family norms
IV. Freedom of the press

Codes

(a) I, II, III and IV
(b) I and II
(c) III and IV
(d) II, III and IV

24. Read the following rights.

I. Right to Equality
II. Right to Freedom
III. Right to Freedom of Religion
IV. Right to Information

Which of the following is not a part of the Part-III of the Constitution?

(a) I (b) II
(c) III (d) IV

25. Consider the following statements and choose the correct option.

I. Right to Property is not a Fundamental Right under the Constitution of India.
II. Right to Property is a legal right.

Codes

(a) Only I
(b) Only II
(c) Both I and II
(d) None of the above

26. There are two statements marked as Assertion (A) and Reason (R). Mark your answer as per the codes given below.

Assertion (A) The state shall provide free and compulsory education to all children of the age group of 6 to 14 years.

Reason (R) In a democratic society, Right to Education is indispensable in the interpretation of the Right to Development as a human right.

Codes

(a) Both A and R are true and R is the correct explanation of A
(b) Both A and R are true, but R is not the correct explanation of A
(c) A is true, but R is false
(d) R is true, but A is false

Darken your choice with HB Pencil

1.	ⓐ ⓑ ⓒ ⓓ	6.	ⓐ ⓑ ⓒ ⓓ	11.	ⓐ ⓑ ⓒ ⓓ	16.	ⓐ ⓑ ⓒ ⓓ	21.	ⓐ ⓑ ⓒ ⓓ	26.	ⓐ ⓑ ⓒ ⓓ
2.	ⓐ ⓑ ⓒ ⓓ	7.	ⓐ ⓑ ⓒ ⓓ	12.	ⓐ ⓑ ⓒ ⓓ	17.	ⓐ ⓑ ⓒ ⓓ	22.	ⓐ ⓑ ⓒ ⓓ		
3.	ⓐ ⓑ ⓒ ⓓ	8.	ⓐ ⓑ ⓒ ⓓ	13.	ⓐ ⓑ ⓒ ⓓ	18.	ⓐ ⓑ ⓒ ⓓ	23.	ⓐ ⓑ ⓒ ⓓ		
4.	ⓐ ⓑ ⓒ ⓓ	9.	ⓐ ⓑ ⓒ ⓓ	14.	ⓐ ⓑ ⓒ ⓓ	19.	ⓐ ⓑ ⓒ ⓓ	24.	ⓐ ⓑ ⓒ ⓓ		
5.	ⓐ ⓑ ⓒ ⓓ	10.	ⓐ ⓑ ⓒ ⓓ	15.	ⓐ ⓑ ⓒ ⓓ	20.	ⓐ ⓑ ⓒ ⓓ	25.	ⓐ ⓑ ⓒ ⓓ		

Chapter 21

Our Government (Executive, Legislative and Judiciary)

MCQs 1 Mark Questions

1. .... is a form of government in which the politicians are elected by the people.
(a) Democracy
(b) Non-Democratic government
(c) Monarchy
(d) Dictatorship

2. Which of the following is the final authority to make laws in India?
(a) President (b) Prime Minister
(c) Parliament (d) Supreme Court

3. Name the state which does not have a Bicameral Legislature.
(a) Bihar (b) Maharashtra
(c) Haryana (d) Uttar Pradesh

4. Which of the following is not a session of Lok Sabha?
(a) Summer session (b) Winter session
(c) Budget session (d) Monsoon session

5. Which of the following is the highest formal authority in India?
(a) President (b) Prime Minister
(c) Chairman of Rajya Sabha
(d) Member of Parliament

6. .... is an institution where the dispute between the citizens and government is finally settled.
(a) Parliament (b) Supreme Court
(c) President House (d) None of these

7. Complete the given analogy.
Executive : Enforcement of laws : : Judiciary : ?
(a) To interpret the laws and settle disputes
(b) To make laws
(c) To conduct elections
(d) None of the above

8. Identify the name of the institution as shown in the image given below.

(a) President House
(b) Parliament of India
(c) Supreme Court of India
(d) None of the above

9. .... is the head of the state.
(a) President (b) Prime Minister
(c) Governor (d) Speaker

10. The President is the Supreme Commander of ....
(a) Defence Forces of India
(b) Supreme Court
(c) States
(d) Council of Ministers

11. The .... is the guardian of Fundamental Rights in India.
(a) High Court (b) Supreme Court
(c) President (d) Citizens

12. Identify the name of the institution as shown in the image given below.

(a) National Museum
(b) Prime Minister Residence
(c) Supreme Court of India
(d) Lok Sabha

13. Choose the incorrectly matched pair.

Constitutional bodies	**Head**
(a) Supreme Court	– Chief Justice
(b) Lok Sabha	– Speaker
(c) Central Government	– Prime Minister
(d) Rajya Sabha	– Governor

14. Who among the following appoints the Prime Minister of India?
(a) Supreme Court (b) President
(c) Citizens (d) Council of Ministers

15. The judges of the Supreme Court is appointed by................. of India.
(a) President (b) Prime Minister
(c) Parliament (d) Chief Justice

16. Which of the following statements about the Prime Minister is correct?
(a) He appoints the Governor of a state.
(b) He is the highest formal authority of India.
(c) He presides over the sittings of Lok Sabha.
(d) He is directly appointed by the people.

17. What is the government formed by an alliance of two or more political parties called?
(a) Coalition government
(b) Cooperative government
(c) Collective government
(d) Constitutional government

18. Lok Sabha has more powers than Rajya Sabha in ....
(a) administrative matters
(b) passing different bills
(c) money matters
(d) None of the above

19. The Council of Ministers is collectively responsible to which of the following?
(a) Prime Minister (b) President
(c) Rajya Sabha (d) Lok Sabha

20. What is the tenure of Lok Sabha?
(a) 3 years (b) 4 years
(c) 5 years (d) 6 years

MCQs 2 Marks Questions

21. Read the following statements and choose the correct option.
I. The President's assent is required for a bill to become a law.
II. The tenure of Rajya Sabha is 4 years.

Codes
(a) Only I
(b) Only II
(c) Both I and II
(d) None of the above

22. Match the following.

List I	List II
A. Rajya Sabha	1. Money Bill
B. Chief Minister	2. Permanent House
C. Lok Sabha	3. Head of the Government

Codes

	A	B	C		A	B	C
(a)	2	3	1	(b)	1	3	2
(c)	2	1	3	(d)	3	2	1

23. Identify the correct option with the help of the given information.

I. He is a Ex-officio Chairperson of the Rajya Sabha.

II. He is the second highest constitutional office in India.

Codes

(a) President (b) Governor

(c) Vice-President (d) Speaker

24. Which of the following statements are correct?

I. The President of India is a nominal head.

II. He/She is directly elected by the citizens of India.

III. He/She holds the office for the term of 5 years.

Codes

(a) I and II (b) II and III

(c) I and III (d) None of these

25. Read the following statements and choose the correct option.

I. The Governor appoints the Chief Minister of a state.

II. The Governor of a state is appointed by the Prime Minister.

III. The Chief Minister is the real executive of the state government.

Codes

(a) I and II (b) I and III

(c) II and III (d) All of these

26. Identify the name of the President with the help of the information given below.

- He was the 11th President of India.
- He is also known as 'People's President' and the 'Missile Man of India'.

(a) Pranab Mukherjee

(b) APJ Abdul Kalam

(c) Ram Nath Kovind

(d) KR Narayan

27. Read the following statements and choose the correct option.

I. The elections are held at an interval of every 5 years in India.

II. India is a union of states.

Codes

(a) Only I (b) Only II

(c) Both I and II (d) None of these

Darken your choice with HB Pencil

1. ⓐ ⓑ ⓒ ⓓ	6. ⓐ ⓑ ⓒ ⓓ	11. ⓐ ⓑ ⓒ ⓓ	16. ⓐ ⓑ ⓒ ⓓ	21. ⓐ ⓑ ⓒ ⓓ	26. ⓐ ⓑ ⓒ ⓓ
2. ⓐ ⓑ ⓒ ⓓ	7. ⓐ ⓑ ⓒ ⓓ	12. ⓐ ⓑ ⓒ ⓓ	17. ⓐ ⓑ ⓒ ⓓ	22. ⓐ ⓑ ⓒ ⓓ	27. ⓐ ⓑ ⓒ ⓓ
3. ⓐ ⓑ ⓒ ⓓ	8. ⓐ ⓑ ⓒ ⓓ	13. ⓐ ⓑ ⓒ ⓓ	18. ⓐ ⓑ ⓒ ⓓ	23. ⓐ ⓑ ⓒ ⓓ	
4. ⓐ ⓑ ⓒ ⓓ	9. ⓐ ⓑ ⓒ ⓓ	14. ⓐ ⓑ ⓒ ⓓ	19. ⓐ ⓑ ⓒ ⓓ	24. ⓐ ⓑ ⓒ ⓓ	
5. ⓐ ⓑ ⓒ ⓓ	10. ⓐ ⓑ ⓒ ⓓ	15. ⓐ ⓑ ⓒ ⓓ	20. ⓐ ⓑ ⓒ ⓓ	25. ⓐ ⓑ ⓒ ⓓ	

Chapter 22

Panchayati Raj Institution

MCQs 1 Mark Questions

1. Identify the name of the elected leader who heads the local self-government institution at the village level.
(a) Sarpanch (b) Panch
(c) Vice-Sarpanch (d) Panchayat Secretary

2. The Panchayati Raj System was adopted in India in the year ....
(a) 1990 (b) 1992
(c) 2000 (d) 2001

3. Complete the given analogy.
Zila Parishad : District level :: Gram Panchayat : ?
(a) Block level (b) Village level
(c) State level (d) National level

4. District Collector is also known as ....
(a) Land Owner (b) Superintendent
(c) District Magistrate (d) Zamindar

5. Which of the following systems is/are established on the basis of the direct election?
(a) Gram Panchayat (b) Block Committee
(c) Zila Parishad (d) Both (b) and (c)

6. Which one of the following states was the first to establish Panchayati Raj system in India?
(a) Rajasthan (b) Maharashtra
(c) Punjab (d) Andhra Pradesh

7. What is/are the function(s) of Gram Panchayat?
(a) Construction and maintenance of water sources
(b) Building schools
(c) Levying and collecting taxes
(d) All of the above

8. Which among the following is the Constitutional Amendment Act on Panchayati Raj Institutions?
(a) 74th Constitutional Amendment Act
(b) 73rd Constitutional Amendment Act
(c) 72nd Constitutional Amendment Act
(d) 70th Constitutional Amendment Act

9. Identify the minimum age prescribed for election as a member of Panchayat.
(a) 21 years (b) 18 years
(c) 25 years (d) 19 years

10. Which one of the following functions is not the concern of local self-government in India?
(a) Public health
(b) Maintenance of public order
(c) Sanitation
(d) Public Utility Services

11. Identify the name of personality who is considered as the architect of Panchayati Raj Institution in India.
(a) Acharya Narendra Deo
(b) Balwant Rai Mehta
(c) GVK Rao (d) LM Singhvi

12. Which of the following articles is related to Panchayati Raj?
(a) Article 243 (b) Article 324
(c) Article 124 (d) Article 73

13. How many posts are reserved for women at all levels in the Panchayati Raj System?
(a) 1/3 (b) 1/2
(c) 2/3 (d) 1/4

MCQs 2 Marks Questions

14. Which of the following statements is/are correct?
I. Panchayati Raj is a system of local self-government.
II. Only aged people of a village can be the head of a Panchayat.

Codes
(a) Only I (b) Only II
(c) Both I and II (d) None of these

15. Read the statements given below and choose the incorrect option.
I. The National Panchayati Raj Day is observed on 24th April.
II. The Constitution of India mandates that the elections of the Panchayati Raj should be held regularly after a gap of 3 years.

Codes
(a) Only I (b) Only II
(c) Both I and II (d) None of these

16. Read the following statements and choose the correct option.
I. The Sarpanch of a Panchayat is also called as Pradhan.
II. The Block Samiti is an intermediate link between the Gram Panchayat and the Zila Parishad.

Codes
(a) Only I
(b) Only II
(c) Both I and II
(d) None of the above

17. Read the given statements and select the option that correctly identifies true (T) and false (F) ones.
I. Panchayati Raj is a system of local self-government with three-tier system.
II. Panchayati Raj is mainly aimed at decentralisation of power to villagers.
III. All the three levels of Gram Panchayati Raj Institutions are elected directly by the people.

Codes

	I	II	III		I	II	III
(a)	T	T	T	(b)	T	T	F
(c)	F	F	T	(d)	T	F	T

18. There are two statements marked as Assertion (A) and Reason (R). Mark your answer as per the codes given below.

Assertion (A) A Gram Panchayat covers a village or group of villages.

Reason (R) The intermediary level body need not be constituted in smaller states.

Codes
(a) Both A and R are true and R is the correct explanation of A
(b) Both A and R are true, but R is not the correct explanation of A
(c) A is true, but R is false
(d) A is false, but R is true

Darken your choice with HB Pencil

1. ⓐ ⓑ ⓒ ⓓ	4. ⓐ ⓑ ⓒ ⓓ	7. ⓐ ⓑ ⓒ ⓓ	10. ⓐ ⓑ ⓒ ⓓ	13. ⓐ ⓑ ⓒ ⓓ	16. ⓐ ⓑ ⓒ ⓓ
2. ⓐ ⓑ ⓒ ⓓ	5. ⓐ ⓑ ⓒ ⓓ	8. ⓐ ⓑ ⓒ ⓓ	11. ⓐ ⓑ ⓒ ⓓ	14. ⓐ ⓑ ⓒ ⓓ	17. ⓐ ⓑ ⓒ ⓓ
3. ⓐ ⓑ ⓒ ⓓ	6. ⓐ ⓑ ⓒ ⓓ	9. ⓐ ⓑ ⓒ ⓓ	12. ⓐ ⓑ ⓒ ⓓ	15. ⓐ ⓑ ⓒ ⓓ	18. ⓐ ⓑ ⓒ ⓓ

Chapter 23

Elections and Politics

MCQs 1 Mark Questions

1. Identify the state with maximum number of constituencies for Lok Sabha.
(a) West Bengal (b) Maharashtra
(c) Uttar Pradesh (d) Madhya Pradesh

2. Which among the following is incorrect feature of election system in India?
(a) Secret voting
(b) Universal Adult Franchise
(c) Communal Electorate
(d) Reservation of seats for Scheduled Caste and Scheduled Tribes

3. Which of the following best resembles a direct democracy?
(a) Discussions in a family event.
(b) Opinions given on a debate show in media.
(c) Election of a class monitor.
(d) Decisions taken by the Gram Sabha.

4. Election Commission, which is responsible for conducting the elections to the Lok Sabha and State Legislative Assemblies comes under which of the following articles of the Constitution?
(a) Article 324 (b) Article 368
(c) Article 32 (d) Article 163

5. Which of the following is not allowed while carrying out election campaign?
(a) Giving money to voters to cast vote for candidates.
(b) Using TV channels.
(c) Door to Door canvassing.
(d) Contacting voters on phone.

6. Who among the following appoints the Chief Election Commissioner of India?
(a) Lok Sabha (b) Prime Minister
(c) President (d) Chief Justice

7. Which of the following types of election system is prescribed by the Constitution for the elections to the Lok Sabha?
(a) First-Past-the-Post system
(b) Single transferable vote system
(c) Semi-proportional system
(d) Proportional system

8. Who among the following recognises the political parties in India?
(a) President
(b) Speaker of Lok Sabha
(c) Election Commission of India
(d) Prime Minister

9. What is an election held for only one constituency to fill the vacancy caused due to the death or resignation of a member called?
(a) Mid-term election (b) General election
(c) By-election (d) None of these

10. Who among the following appoints the delimitation commission in India?
(a) Election Commission of India
(b) Supreme Court of India
(c) The Parliament
(d) The President

11. Which among the following is incorrect about Election Commission?
(a) The Election Commission conducts all elections for the Parliament and Assemblies.
(b) The Election Commission directs and controls the preparation of electoral roll.
(c) The Election Commission cannot fix the election dates.
(d) The Election Commission does scrutiny of nomination papers.

12. What is the age requirement for the candidate to contest the Lok Sabha elections?
(a) 18 years (b) 25 years
(c) 30 years (d) 21 years

13. Which of the following provisions can make elections free and fair?
(a) Universal Adult Franchise
(b) Independent Election Commission
(c) Both (a) and (b)
(d) Communal electorate

14. Which of the following statements is/are the function(s) of the political party?
(a) They put forward different policies and programmes.
(b) Parties are not very effective in shaping public opinion.
(c) Parties form and run government.
(d) Both (a) and (c)

15. What does VVPAT stands for in the context of elections?
(a) Voter Verified Paper Audit Trial
(b) Voter Verifiable Paper Auditing Technology
(c) Voter Verified Paper Authentication Technique
(d) Voter Verifiable Paper Audit Trial

16. Name the body who decides the disputes regarding election of President of India.
(a) Supreme Court
(b) Election Commission
(c) Parliament
(d) High Court

17. Complete the given analogy.
Bharatiya Janata Party : National Party : : ? : State Party
(a) Indian National Congress
(b) Communist Party of India
(c) Samajwadi Party
(d) Bahujan Samaj Party

18. Which of the following countries has/have adopted multi-party system?
(a) India (b) Canada
(c) Both (a) and (b) (d) United Kingdom

19. Identify the political party whose symbol is represented in the image given below.

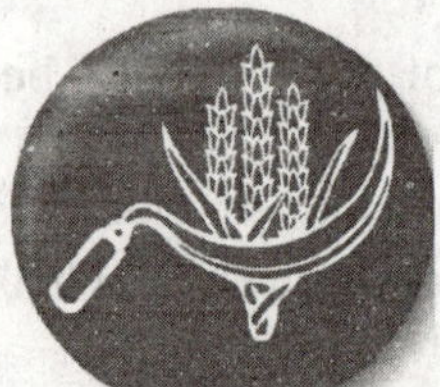

(a) Communist Party of India
(b) All India Trinamool Congress
(c) Shiromani Akali Dal
(d) Sikkim Democratic Front

20. Which of the following Constitutional Amendment Acts reduced the voting age from 21 years to 18 years?
(a) 63rd Constitutional Amendment Act
(b) 62nd Constitutional Amendment Act
(c) 61st Constitutional Amendment Act
(d) 64th Constitutional Amendment Act

21. Indian National Congress was formed in which of the following years?

(a) 1947 (b) 1885

(c) 1935 (d) 1858

MCQs 2 Marks Questions

22. Consider the following statements and choose the correct option.

I. The founder of the Bahujan Samaj Party is Dr BR Ambedkar.

II. A group of people who come together to contest elections and hold power in the government is called a political party.

Codes

(a) Only I (b) Both I and II

(c) Only II (d) Neither I nor II

23. Match the following.

List I (Political Party)	List II (Type of Party)
A. Bahujan Samaj Party	1. Left-wing Party
B. Communist Party of India (Marxist)	2. Regional party
C. Telugu Desam Party	3. National party

Codes

	A	B	C		A	B	C
(a)	2	3	1	(b)	3	2	1
(c)	2	1	3	(d)	3	1	2

24. Consider the following statements on political parties.

I. Political parties nominate candidates for elections.

II. Political parties conduct elections to Legislature.

III. Political parties present manifestos to affirm their agenda and goals.

Which of the above statements is/are correct?

(a) I and III (b) I and II

(c) I, II and III (d) Only II

25. Consider the following statements and choose the correct option.

I. Election Commission of India is a multi member body.

II. It consists of one Chief Election Commission and two other Election Commissioner.

Codes

(a) Only I (b) Only II

(c) Both I and II (d) Neither I nor II

26. There are two statements marked as Assertion (A) and Reason (R). Mark your answer as per the codes given below.

Assertion (A) The State Election Commission is a Constitutional Authority.

Reason (R) Elections to rural local bodies are overseen by the Election Commission of India.

Codes

(a) Both A and R are true and R is the correct explanation of A

(b) Both A and R are true, but R is not the correct explanation of A

(c) A is true, but R is false

(d) A is false, but R is true

Darken your choice with HB Pencil

1. ⓐ ⓑ ⓒ ⓓ	6. ⓐ ⓑ ⓒ ⓓ	11. ⓐ ⓑ ⓒ ⓓ	16. ⓐ ⓑ ⓒ ⓓ	21. ⓐ ⓑ ⓒ ⓓ	26. ⓐ ⓑ ⓒ ⓓ
2. ⓐ ⓑ ⓒ ⓓ	7. ⓐ ⓑ ⓒ ⓓ	12. ⓐ ⓑ ⓒ ⓓ	17. ⓐ ⓑ ⓒ ⓓ	22. ⓐ ⓑ ⓒ ⓓ	
3. ⓐ ⓑ ⓒ ⓓ	8. ⓐ ⓑ ⓒ ⓓ	13. ⓐ ⓑ ⓒ ⓓ	18. ⓐ ⓑ ⓒ ⓓ	23. ⓐ ⓑ ⓒ ⓓ	
4. ⓐ ⓑ ⓒ ⓓ	9. ⓐ ⓑ ⓒ ⓓ	14. ⓐ ⓑ ⓒ ⓓ	19. ⓐ ⓑ ⓒ ⓓ	24. ⓐ ⓑ ⓒ ⓓ	
5. ⓐ ⓑ ⓒ ⓓ	10. ⓐ ⓑ ⓒ ⓓ	15. ⓐ ⓑ ⓒ ⓓ	20. ⓐ ⓑ ⓒ ⓓ	25. ⓐ ⓑ ⓒ ⓓ	

Chapter 24

Science and Technology

MCQs 1 Mark Questions

1. Nuclear fusion takes place in which of the following states of matter?
(a) Solid (b) Gas
(c) Plasma (d) Liquid

2. Which Indian satellite is Intended for long distance telecommunication for transmitting TV programmes?
(a) Rohini (b) Aryabhatta
(c) Bhaskara (d) INSAT-A

3. High speed neutrons are required to carry out which of the following reactions?
(a) Nuclear fusion (b) Nuclear fission
(c) Both (a) and (b) (d) None of these

4. Which of the following informations can be obtained using geospatial technology?
(a) Vegetation cover of any country
(b) Traffic on the road
(c) Information relating to earthquake
(d) All of the above

5. Who among the following invented the Crescograph, an instrument which demonstrated the minute movements of plants and measure their rate of growth?
(a) JC Bose
(b) Srinivas Ramanujan
(c) Satyendranath Bose
(d) PC Mahalanobis

6. Which of the following statements is true with respect to electromagnetic energy?
(a) This energy travels in waves.
(b) It spans a very narrow spectrum with only limited wave length.
(c) Human eye can detect only infrared portion of this spectrum.
(d) Radio waves are not a part of electromagnetic spectrum.

7. Complete the given analogy.
ISRO : Bengaluru : : DRDO : ?
(a) New Delhi (b) Mumbai
(c) Pune (d) Nagpur

8. Which of the following has the highest wave length in the electromagnetic spectrum as compared to the other three?
(a) Infrared (b) Visible
(c) Ultraviolet (d) X-rays

9. Identify the name of personality, who is popularly called as the Father of Indian Space Program.
(a) Vikram Sarabhai
(b) Hargovind Khurrana
(c) APJ Abdul Kalam
(d) CV Raman

10. Which of the following is also known as unmanned aerial vehicle?
(a) Helicopters (b) Satellite
(c) Drone (d) Rocket

11. Where is the kupier belt located?
(a) Beyond the orbit of Neptune
(b) Between Mars and Jupiter
(c) Between Venus and Earth
(d) None of the above

12. Which was the first spacecraft to successfully land on the Moon?
(a) Chandrayan (b) Apollo
(c) Luna (d) Chang's

13. Which one of the following refers to the first nuclear reactor to India?
(a) Kamini (b) Apsara
(c) Urvashi (d) Rohini

14. Identify the name of country which launched the first satellite 'Sputnik' into the space.
(a) USSR (b) USA
(c) United Kingdom (d) China

15. Which of the following actions can lead to antibiotic resistance?
(a) Taking antibiotics on regular time.
(b) Not completing the five day course of an antibiotic during flu.
(c) Grinding the antibiotic tablet before ingesting.
(d) Ingestion of antibiotics with hot water.

16. Which of the following is not an example of antibiotic?
(a) Penicillin (b) Azithromycin
(c) Paracetamol (d) Amoxicillin

17. Which of the following metals is mainly used in electric vehicle batteries?
(a) Copper (b) Aluminium
(c) Tin (d) Lithium

18. Complete the given analogy.
Hepatitis : Communicable disease : : ? : Non-Communicable disease
(a) HIV (b) Tuberculosis
(c) Cancer (d) Measles

19. Mycobacterium tuberculosis bacteria mainly affects which of the following organs?
(a) Heart
(b) Lungs
(c) Salivary glands
(d) Urethra

20. What is the full form of CSIR?
(a) Council of Scientists , Inventors and Researchers
(b) Council of Scientific and Industrial Research
(c) Council of Space Inventions and Reasearch
(d) Council of Space Industry and Research

21. Which of the following habits doesn't strengthen the immune system?
(a) Regular sleep
(b) Skipping meals
(c) Intake of vitamins
(d) Regular exercise

22. Which of the following is not true with regard to vaccines?
(a) They help to fight diseases.
(b) They stimulates immune response.
(c) They provide passive immunity.
(d) They contain weakened form of disease causing organism.

23. What does the code name 'Smiling Buddha' denotes?
(a) First nuclear test
(b) First satellite mission
(c) First Buddhist site discovery
(d) First Buddhist monastery discovery

24. .... is the first permanent base station of India in Antarctica.
(a) Bharat Veer
(b) Godavari
(c) Sugandha
(d) Dakshingangotri

MCQs 2 Marks Questions

25. Consider the following statements and choose the correct option.

I. Edward Jenner created the world's first successful vaccine.

II. The first vaccine was developed for chicken pox.

Codes

(a) Both I and II (b) Only I
(c) Only II (d) Neither I nor II

26. Match the following.

	List I (Planets)		List II (Position from the Sun)
A.	Jupiter	1.	First
B.	Mercury	2.	Eight
C.	Uranus	3.	Seventh
D.	Neptune	4.	Fifth

Codes

	A	B	C	D		A	B	C	D
(a)	3	2	1	4	(b)	2	1	3	4
(c)	4	3	1	2	(d)	4	1	3	2

27. Consider the following statements and choose the correct option.

I. Satellites can be used for educational purposes, but not for agricultural purposes.

II. Unmanned aerial vehicles can be used for agricultural purposes.

Codes

(a) Only I
(b) Both I and II
(c) Neither I nor II
(d) Only II

28. There are two statements marked as Assertion (A) and Reason (R). Mark your answer as per the codes given below.

Assertion (A) GPS technology can be used widely for location services.

Reason (R) GPS uses satellites for providing services.

Codes

(a) Both A and R are true and R is the correct explanation of A
(b) Both A and R are true, but R is not the correct explanation of A
(c) A is true, but R is false
(d) A is false, but R is true

29. Which of the following are included under the information and communication technology?

I. Satellites II. Computers
III. Thermometer IV. Electronic kettle

Codes

(a) II and IV (b) I, II, III and IV
(c) I and II (d) I, II and IV

30. There are two statements marked as Assertion (A) and Reason (R). Mark your answer as per the codes given below.

Assertion (A) Robots can do some tasks which even a real human beings cannot do.

Reason (R) Robots are developed using artificial intelligence.

Codes

(a) Both A and R are true and R is the correct explanation of A
(b) Both A and R are true, but R is not the correct explanation of A
(c) A is true, but R is false
(d) A is false, but R is true

Darken your choice with HB Pencil

1. ⓐ ⓑ ⓒ ⓓ	6. ⓐ ⓑ ⓒ ⓓ	11. ⓐ ⓑ ⓒ ⓓ	16. ⓐ ⓑ ⓒ ⓓ	21. ⓐ ⓑ ⓒ ⓓ	26. ⓐ ⓑ ⓒ ⓓ
2. ⓐ ⓑ ⓒ ⓓ	7. ⓐ ⓑ ⓒ ⓓ	12. ⓐ ⓑ ⓒ ⓓ	17. ⓐ ⓑ ⓒ ⓓ	22. ⓐ ⓑ ⓒ ⓓ	27. ⓐ ⓑ ⓒ ⓓ
3. ⓐ ⓑ ⓒ ⓓ	8. ⓐ ⓑ ⓒ ⓓ	13. ⓐ ⓑ ⓒ ⓓ	18. ⓐ ⓑ ⓒ ⓓ	23. ⓐ ⓑ ⓒ ⓓ	28. ⓐ ⓑ ⓒ ⓓ
4. ⓐ ⓑ ⓒ ⓓ	9. ⓐ ⓑ ⓒ ⓓ	14. ⓐ ⓑ ⓒ ⓓ	19. ⓐ ⓑ ⓒ ⓓ	24. ⓐ ⓑ ⓒ ⓓ	29. ⓐ ⓑ ⓒ ⓓ
5. ⓐ ⓑ ⓒ ⓓ	10. ⓐ ⓑ ⓒ ⓓ	15. ⓐ ⓑ ⓒ ⓓ	20. ⓐ ⓑ ⓒ ⓓ	25. ⓐ ⓑ ⓒ ⓓ	30. ⓐ ⓑ ⓒ ⓓ

Chapter 25

Sports

MCQs 1 Mark Questions

1. What is the full form of ICC?
(a) Indian Cricket Council
(b) International Cricket Council
(c) International Cricket Code
(d) Indian Cricket Code

2. The FIFA Football World Cup is normally held every ………… year.
(a) four (b) two
(c) three (d) one

3. The term 'Red Card' is associated with which of the following sports?
(a) Volleyball
(b) Football
(c) Basketball
(d) Baseball

4. Complete the given analogy.
Boxing : Ring :: Badminton : ?
(a) Court (b) Field
(c) Mat (d) Pitch

5. Which of the following sportspersons is also known as 'Dhing Express'?
(a) PT Usha
(b) Jwala Gutta
(c) Saina Nehwal
(d) Hima Das

6. The footballer Maradona belonged to which of the following countries?
(a) Peru (b) Chile
(c) Argentina (d) Italy

7. Which of the following sportspersons is also called 'Golden Girl' or 'Payyoli Express'?
(a) Saina Nehwal (b) PT Usha
(c) Sania Mirza (d) Dipa Karmakar

8. Mithali Raj is associated with which of the following sports?
(a) Cricket (b) Hockey
(c) Basketball (d) Wrestling

9. Identify the incorrectly matched pair.

	Sportsperson		Associated sport
(a)	Mithali Raj	–	Cricket
(b)	Neeraj Chopra	–	Boxing
(c)	Sushil Kumar	–	Wrestling
(d)	Rohan Bopanna	–	Tennis

10. Identify the name of country which is considered as the 'Father of Cricket'.
(a) India (b) England
(c) USA (d) China

11. The terms LBW and No Ball is associated with ………… .
(a) volleyball (b) football
(c) hockey (d) cricket

12. In which of the following cities, does the Arun Jaitley Cricket Stadium situated?
(a) Delhi (b) Mumbai
(c) Kolkata (d) Chennai

13. Name the highest governing body of table tennis sport.
(a) International Table Tennis Federation
(b) International Table Tennis Association
(c) International Table Tennis Committee
(d) International Table Tennis Organisation

14. The BCCI is associated with which of the following sports?
(a) Hockey (b) Chess
(c) Cricket (d) Wrestling

15. Complete the given analogy.
Flying Sikh : Milkha Singh :: Haryana Hurricane : ?
(a) Sunil Gavaskar (b) Kapil Dev
(c) Yuvraj Singh (d) Bajrang Punia

16. The terms French Open, Wimbledon and Australian Open are associated with ……………… .
(a) badminton (b) tennis
(c) table tennis (d) hockey

17. Identify the name of the player associated with tennis.

(a) Rafael Nadal
(b) Novak Djokovic
(c) Roger Federer
(d) Pete Sampras

18. Which of the following cities is going to host Summer Olympics of 2024?
(a) Paris (b) Shanghai
(c) New Delhi (d) New York

19. The Uber Cup is associated with which of the following sports?
(a) Cricket (b) Football
(c) Badminton (d) Chess

20. Choose the incorrectly matched pair.

	Sports		**Cups/ Trophies**
(a)	Hockey	–	Aga Khan Cup
(b)	Football	–	Ashutosh Trophy
(c)	Chess	–	Ranji Trophy
(d)	Boat Race	–	Nehru Trophy

21. The term 'Gambit' is associated with ……………
(a) chess (b) baseball
(c) football (d) hockey

MCQs 2 Marks Questions

22. Read the following statements and choose the correct option.
I. Neeraj Chopra is a well known chess Grandmaster of India.
II. Rahul Dravid is also known as 'The Wall' of the Indian Cricket Team.

Codes
(a) Only I (b) Only II
(c) Both I and II (d) None of these

23. Match the following.

List I (Country)	**List II** (National Games)
A. Japan	1. Football
B. England	2. Baseball
C. France	3. Sumo Wrestling
D. USA	4. Cricket

Codes

	A	B	C	D		A	B	C	D
(a)	1	3	4	2	(b)	3	4	1	2
(c)	4	2	1	3	(d)	2	3	4	1

24. Identify the name of the player with the help of the information given below.

- She is the only woman to win the World Amateur Boxing Championship six times.
- She hails from the state of Manipur and was honoured with Padma Vibhushan in the year 2020.

(a) Sarita Devi (b) Lovlina Borgohain
(c) Mary Kom (d) Nikhat Zareen

25. Read the following statements and select the option that correctly identifies true (T) and false (F) ones.

I. Cricket is the national sports of India.
II. Major Dhyan Chand is associated with Ice Skating.
III. There are total 10 players in each hockey team.
IV. Eden Garden Stadium is located in the state of West Bengal.

Codes

	I	II	III	IV		I	II	III	IV
(a)	F	F	F	T	(b)	T	T	T	T
(c)	F	F	T	T	(d)	T	F	T	F

26. Read the following statements and choose the correct option.

I. Wankhede Stadium is related to hockey.
II. M Chinnaswamy Stadium is a cricket stadium located in Bangalore.
III. Narendra Modi Stadium is the largest cricket stadium in the world.

Codes

(a) I and II (b) II and III
(c) I and III (d) All of these

27. Match the following.

List I (Sports)	List II (Country of Origin)
A. Chess	1. England
B. Cricket	2. India
C. Tennis	3. Canada
D. Ice Hockey	4. France

Codes

	A	B	C	D		A	B	C	D
(a)	2	1	4	3	(b)	1	2	3	4
(c)	4	1	3	2	(d)	2	3	4	1

28. Identify the name of the sport with the help of the given information.

- The traditional sport is celebrated on the 3rd day of Pongal.
- It is practiced in the state of Tamil Nadu.

(a) Wrestling (b) Jallikattu
(c) Mallakhamb (d) Kambala

29. Which of the following statements are correct?

I. In football, the field is rectangular in shape.
II. In archery, the shape of the target is square.
III. The term ODI is related to domestic cricket matches.
IV. Serena Williams is associated with tennis.

Codes

(a) I and III (b) I, II and IV
(c) I and IV (d) All of these

Darken your choice with HB Pencil

1. ⓐ ⓑ ⓒ ⓓ	6. ⓐ ⓑ ⓒ ⓓ	11. ⓐ ⓑ ⓒ ⓓ	16. ⓐ ⓑ ⓒ ⓓ	21. ⓐ ⓑ ⓒ ⓓ	26. ⓐ ⓑ ⓒ ⓓ
2. ⓐ ⓑ ⓒ ⓓ	7. ⓐ ⓑ ⓒ ⓓ	12. ⓐ ⓑ ⓒ ⓓ	17. ⓐ ⓑ ⓒ ⓓ	22. ⓐ ⓑ ⓒ ⓓ	27. ⓐ ⓑ ⓒ ⓓ
3. ⓐ ⓑ ⓒ ⓓ	8. ⓐ ⓑ ⓒ ⓓ	13. ⓐ ⓑ ⓒ ⓓ	18. ⓐ ⓑ ⓒ ⓓ	23. ⓐ ⓑ ⓒ ⓓ	28. ⓐ ⓑ ⓒ ⓓ
4. ⓐ ⓑ ⓒ ⓓ	9. ⓐ ⓑ ⓒ ⓓ	14. ⓐ ⓑ ⓒ ⓓ	19. ⓐ ⓑ ⓒ ⓓ	24. ⓐ ⓑ ⓒ ⓓ	29. ⓐ ⓑ ⓒ ⓓ
5. ⓐ ⓑ ⓒ ⓓ	10. ⓐ ⓑ ⓒ ⓓ	15. ⓐ ⓑ ⓒ ⓓ	20. ⓐ ⓑ ⓒ ⓓ	25. ⓐ ⓑ ⓒ ⓓ	

Chapter 26

Awards, Honours and Recognitions

MCQs 1 Mark Questions

1. The Pulitzer Award was instituted in the year ....
(a) 1917 (b) 1918
(c) 1919 (d) 1920

2. Which among the following awards is the highest Civilian Award of India?
(a) Padma Shri (b) Padma Vibhushan
(c) Bharat Ratna (d) Ashoka Chakra

3. Who was the first Indian to receive the Magsaysay Award?
(a) Indira Gandhi (b) Kiran Bedi
(c) TN Seshan (d) Vinoba Bhave

4. Complete the given analogy.
IIFA Awards : Cinema :: Grammy Awards : ?
(a) Medical Science (b) Sports
(c) Agriculture (d) Music

5. Which of the following personalities is the first Indian and also the first Asian to be honoured with a Nobel Prize?
(a) Rabindranath Tagore
(b) Kailash Satyarthi
(c) Amartya Sen
(d) V Ramakrishnan

6. Who was the first lady recipient of Dada Saheb Phalke Award?
(a) Devika Rani
(b) Uma Devi
(c) Nargis Dutt
(d) Sulochana

7. Choose the incorrectly matched pair.

Award/Prize		Field
(a) Pulitzer	–	Journalism and Literature
(b) Arjuna	–	Sports
(c) Oscar	–	Film
(d) Nobel	–	Agriculture

8. Identify the name of award with the help of the image given below.

(a) Bharat Ratna
(b) Dronacharya Award
(c) Rajiv Gandhi Khel Ratna Award
(d) Arjuna Award

9. The first musician to be felicitated with a 'Bharat Ratna' was ....
(a) Pt Ravi Shankar (b) MS Subbulakshmi
(c) Lata Mangeshkar (d) Pt Bhimsen Joshi

10. Which among the following awards is the highest Gallantry Award of India?
(a) Param Vishisht Seva Medal
(b) Param Vir Chakra
(c) Kirti Chakra
(d) Vir Chakra

11. Amartya Sen was awarded the Nobel Prize for his contribution in ....
(a) Econometrics
(b) Welfare Economics
(c) Monetary Economics
(d) Development Economics

12. The Shanti Swarup Bhatnagar award is given for which among the following fields?
(a) Film (b) Music
(c) Science (d) Journalism

13. The first recipient of Rajiv Gandhi (Dhyan Chand) Khel Ratna award is ....
(a) Vishwanathan Anand (b) Leander Peas
(c) Yuvraj Singh (d) Milkha Singh

14. Which is the highest literary award of the world?
(a) Booker Prize (b) Pulitzer Prize
(c) Nobel Prize (d) Magsaysay Award

15. Identify the name of the award shown in the image which is related to cinema.

(a) Dada Saheb Phalke Award
(b) Oscar Award
(c) Filmfare Award
(d) Magsaysay Award

16. Complete the given analogy.
Sahitya Akademi Award : Literature :: Lalit Kala Akademi Award ?
(a) Music
(b) Literature
(c) Peace
(d) Fine Arts

17. .... award is given in the field of Medical Science.
(a) Dhanwantari
(b) Juliet Curie Award
(c) Pampa Award
(d) Awadh Samman

18. Who among the following confers the Gallantry awards for the distinguished services in India?
(a) Prime Minister
(b) President
(c) Lok Sabha Speaker
(d) Vice-President

19. Dada Saheb Phalke Award is given for the outstanding contribution in the field of ....
(a) Cinema
(b) Literature
(c) Architecture
(d) Medical Science

20. Choose the incorrectly matched pair.

Awards	Country of origin
(a) Nobel Prize	– Sweden
(b) Oscar	– USA
(c) Ramon Magsaysay Award	– Philippines
(d) Booker Prize	– Australia

21. Who was the first foreigner to win the Bharat Ratna?

(a) Khan Abdul Ghaffar Khan
(b) Benazir Bhutto
(c) Winston Churchill
(d) Nelson Mandela

22. The 'Jnanpith Award' is the highest award given for .... by the Bharatiya Jnanpith Trust.

(a) learning and encouraging social peace
(b) literature
(c) banking
(d) economy

23. Which city bagged the first position in Cleanest City of India Award of Swachhta Survekshan many times?

(a) Mumbai (b) Bengaluru
(c) Indore (d) Kolkata

24. Identify the incorrectly matched pair.

	Award		Field
(a)	Bihari Samman	–	Literature
(b)	Dronacharya Award	–	Sports Coach
(c)	Tansen Award	–	Music
(d)	Kabir Samman	–	Peace

MCQs 2 Mark Questions

25. Arrange the following Civilian Awards in ascending degree of honour.

I. Bharat Ratna
II. Padma Vibhushan
III. Padma Bhushan
IV. Padma Shri

Codes

(a) II, III, I, IV
(b) IV, III, II, I
(c) I, III, II, IV
(d) IV, II, III, I

26. Identify the name of the Oscar winner with the help of the information given below.

- He is an Indian social reformer who campaigned against the child labour in India.
- He also initiated the 'Bachpan Bachao Andolan'.

(a) Satyajit Ray
(b) Kailash Satyarthi
(c) Bhanu Athaiya
(d) None of the above

27. Consider the following statements regarding awards and choose the correct option.

I. UNESCO Peace Prize is given for extraordinary contributions for international peace.
II. UNESCO Peace Prize was established in 1989 and presented by United Nations Educational, Scientific and Culture Organisations (UNESCO).

Codes

(a) Only I
(b) Only II
(c) Both I and II
(d) Neither I nor II

Darken your choice with HB Pencil

1.	ⓐ ⓑ ⓒ ⓓ	6.	ⓐ ⓑ ⓒ ⓓ	11.	ⓐ ⓑ ⓒ ⓓ	16.	ⓐ ⓑ ⓒ ⓓ	21.	ⓐ ⓑ ⓒ ⓓ	26.	ⓐ ⓑ ⓒ ⓓ
2.	ⓐ ⓑ ⓒ ⓓ	7.	ⓐ ⓑ ⓒ ⓓ	12.	ⓐ ⓑ ⓒ ⓓ	17.	ⓐ ⓑ ⓒ ⓓ	22.	ⓐ ⓑ ⓒ ⓓ	27.	ⓐ ⓑ ⓒ ⓓ
3.	ⓐ ⓑ ⓒ ⓓ	8.	ⓐ ⓑ ⓒ ⓓ	13.	ⓐ ⓑ ⓒ ⓓ	18.	ⓐ ⓑ ⓒ ⓓ	23.	ⓐ ⓑ ⓒ ⓓ		
4.	ⓐ ⓑ ⓒ ⓓ	9.	ⓐ ⓑ ⓒ ⓓ	14.	ⓐ ⓑ ⓒ ⓓ	19.	ⓐ ⓑ ⓒ ⓓ	24.	ⓐ ⓑ ⓒ ⓓ		
5.	ⓐ ⓑ ⓒ ⓓ	10.	ⓐ ⓑ ⓒ ⓓ	15.	ⓐ ⓑ ⓒ ⓓ	20.	ⓐ ⓑ ⓒ ⓓ	25.	ⓐ ⓑ ⓒ ⓓ		

Chapter 27

General Science

MCQs 1 Mark Questions

1. Which of the following is not a property of a metal?
   (a) Malleablity (b) Ductility
   (c) Lusture (d) Bad Conductance

2. Which metal remains in a liquid state at room temperature?
   (a) Copper (b) Gold
   (c) Mercury (d) Iron

3. Which of the following bacteria is responsible for nitrogen fixation?
   (a) Pseudomonas (b) Rhizobium
   (c) Lactobacillus (d) Norovirus

4. Complete the given analogy.
   Goitre : Iodine deficiency :: Anaemia : ?
   (a) Calcium deficiency
   (b) Iron deficiency
   (c) Vitamin deficiency
   (d) Protein deficiency

5. .... is commonly known as laughing gas.
   (a) Nitrous oxide
   (b) Carbon dioxide
   (c) Oxygen
   (d) Helium

6. ISRO was formed on 15th August, 1969 and related to ....
   (a) defence and security
   (b) flora and fauna
   (c) space and technology
   (d) robotics

7. Milk, eggs, cheese, yogurt and fish are rich source of ....
   (a) carbohydrates (b) sugar
   (c) calcium (d) Vitamin C

8. Complete the given analogy.
   Missile Man of India : Dr Abdul Kalam :: Father of Indian Space Programme : ?
   (a) CV Raman (b) Vikram Sarabhai
   (c) K Sivan (d) None of these

9. Complete the given analogy.
   Kidney : Epithelial tissue : : Bone : ?
   (a) Protective tissue
   (b) Permanent tissue
   (c) Connective tissue
   (d) Muscular tissue

10. The process of splitting of light into its colours is known as ....
    (a) diffusion (b) dispersion
    (c) refraction (d) None of these

11. Identify the type of plant with the help of the image given below.

(a) Autotrophs (b) Insectivorous
(c) Saprophytes (d) None of these

12. The Ozone layer is located in the .... of Earth.
(a) troposphere (b) stratosphere
(c) exosphere (d) mesosphere

13. Consider the following statements and choose the incorrect option.
(a) The fertilisers are commercially produced plant nutrients.
(b) The Pashmina wool is obtained from Kashmiri goat.
(c) Neither (a) nor (b)
(d) Both (a) and (b)

14. Acid turns blue litmus paper into which colour?
(a) Black (b) Blue
(c) Red (d) Orange

15. Which one of the following is not the unit of energy?
(a) Joule
(b) Newton metre
(c) Kilometre
(d) Kilowatt hour

16. According to Newton's Second Law of Motion, change in momentum per unit time is equal to ....
(a) force (b) energy
(c) acceleration (d) work

17. Which device is used to measure earthquakes?
(a) Seismograph (b) Odometer
(c) Barometer (d) Voltmeter

18. What is the unit of wavelength?
(a) Hertz (b) Diopter
(c) Faraday (d) Meter

19. .... is used to measure the purity of the milk.
(a) Ammeter (b) Hygrometer
(c) Lactometer (d) Thermometer

20. Which of the following processes directly converts solid into gas?
(a) Sublimation (b) Evaporation
(c) Transpiration (d) Vapourisation

21. Which of the following is not a chemical change?
(a) Boiling of water (b) Milk turning sour
(c) Ripening of fruits (d) Rusting of iron

22. Sodium bicarbonate is commercially known as ....
(a) vinegar (b) baking soda
(c) bleaching powder (d) washing powder

23. Which of these is/are used as a material for making semi-conductor devices?
(a) Silicon (b) Germanium
(c) Gallium Arsenide (d) All of these

MCQs 2 Marks Questions

24. Match the following.

	List I (Disease)	List I (Organs affected)
A.	Rickets	1. Liver
B.	Tuberculosis	2. Heart
C.	Cardiac arrest	3. Bones
D.	Jaundice	4. Lungs

Codes

	A	B	C	D
(a)	3	4	2	1
(b)	1	3	4	2
(c)	2	1	3	4
(d)	1	2	3	4

25. Read the following statements and choose the correct option.

I. E Rutherford was the discoverer of electron.

II. JJ Thomson gave the 'Theory of Relativity'.

Codes

(a) Only I (b) Only II

(c) Both I and II (d) None of these

26. Which of the following statements are correct?

I. Bronze is an alloy of copper and tin.

II. Acetic acid is commonly known as vinegar.

III. Curd tastes sour due to the presence of lactic acid.

Codes

(a) I and III (b) II and III

(c) I and II (d) All of these

27. Identify the following process with the help of the information given below.

- It is the process by which plants use sunlight, water and carbon dioxide to create energy in the form of sugar.
- The process is carried out mainly by green plants.

(a) Photosynthesis (b) Precipitation

(c) Carbon cycle (d) Nitrogen cycle

28. Read the following statements and choose the correct option.

I. The symbol of Gold is 'Au'.

II. When a gas is turned into a liquid, the process is called condensation.

III. The isotopes have same atomic number but different mass number.

Codes

(a) I and III

(b) II and III

(c) I and II

(d) All of the above

29. There are two statements marked as Assertion (A) and Reason (R). Mark your answer as per the codes given below.

Assertion (A) Mixed cropping is growing two or more crops simultaneously on the same piece of land.

Reason (R) Inter-cropping is growing two or more crops simultaneously on the same field in a definite pattern.

Codes

(a) Both A and R are true and R is the correct explanation of A

(b) Both A and R are true, but R is not the correct explanation of A

(c) A is true, but R is false

(d) A is false, but R is true

Darken your choice with HB Pencil

1.	ⓐ ⓑ ⓒ ⓓ	6.	ⓐ ⓑ ⓒ ⓓ	11.	ⓐ ⓑ ⓒ ⓓ	16.	ⓐ ⓑ ⓒ ⓓ	21.	ⓐ ⓑ ⓒ ⓓ	26.	ⓐ ⓑ ⓒ ⓓ
2.	ⓐ ⓑ ⓒ ⓓ	7.	ⓐ ⓑ ⓒ ⓓ	12.	ⓐ ⓑ ⓒ ⓓ	17.	ⓐ ⓑ ⓒ ⓓ	22.	ⓐ ⓑ ⓒ ⓓ	27.	ⓐ ⓑ ⓒ ⓓ
3.	ⓐ ⓑ ⓒ ⓓ	8.	ⓐ ⓑ ⓒ ⓓ	13.	ⓐ ⓑ ⓒ ⓓ	18.	ⓐ ⓑ ⓒ ⓓ	23.	ⓐ ⓑ ⓒ ⓓ	28.	ⓐ ⓑ ⓒ ⓓ
4.	ⓐ ⓑ ⓒ ⓓ	9.	ⓐ ⓑ ⓒ ⓓ	14.	ⓐ ⓑ ⓒ ⓓ	19.	ⓐ ⓑ ⓒ ⓓ	24.	ⓐ ⓑ ⓒ ⓓ	29.	ⓐ ⓑ ⓒ ⓓ
5.	ⓐ ⓑ ⓒ ⓓ	10.	ⓐ ⓑ ⓒ ⓓ	15.	ⓐ ⓑ ⓒ ⓓ	20.	ⓐ ⓑ ⓒ ⓓ	25.	ⓐ ⓑ ⓒ ⓓ		

Chapter 28

General Awareness

(Books & Authors, Abbreviations, Capital & Currencies, Miscellaneous)

MCQs 1 Mark Questions

1. Which of the following leaders has authored the book 'Hind Swaraj'?
   (a) Bhagat Singh
   (b) Mahatma Gandhi
   (c) Chandra Shekhar Azad
   (d) Bal Gangadhar Tilak

2. Who among the following wrote the book 'An Autobiography'?
   (a) Bhagat Singh
   (b) Mahatma Gandhi
   (c) Jawaharlal Nehru
   (d) Subhash Chandra Bose

3. Who among the following is the author of 'Malgudi Days'?
   (a) RK Narayan
   (b) Vishnu Sharma
   (c) Chetan Bhagat
   (d) Salman Rushdie

4. Identify the name of the writer of 'The Discovery of India'.
   (a) Madan Mohan Malviya
   (b) Bal Gangadhar Tilak
   (c) Jawaharlal Nehru
   (d) Mahatma Gandhi

5. Identify the incorrectly matched pair.

	Author		Books
(a)	JK Rowling	–	Harry Potter
(b)	Premchand	–	Godan
(c)	Anne Frank	–	Diary of a Young Girl
(d)	Rabindranath Tagore	–	Anandamath

6. Who is the writer of the autobiography 'My Experiments with Truth'?
   (a) Sardar Vallabhbhai Patel
   (b) Mahatma Gandhi
   (c) Chandra Shekhar Azad
   (d) Bipin Chandra Pal

7. Identify the name of the book with the help of the image given below.

   (a) Gulliver's Travels
   (b) Alice in Wonderland
   (c) Malgudi Days
   (d) Arabian Nights

8. What is the full form of BRICS?
(a) Britain Russia Indonesia China Sudan
(b) Brazil Rome India China Argentina
(c) Brazil Russia India China South Africa
(d) Belarus Romania Italy Cambodia Spain

9. Complete the given analogy.
ICAR : Agriculture :: AIIMS : ?
(a) Economics
(b) Wildlife
(c) Medical Science
(d) Disaster Management

10. What is the full form of FAO?
(a) Food and Agricultural Organisation
(b) Foreigner's Administrative Organisation
(c) Food Authority Organisation
(d) Family and Amusements

11. Cape Town is the capital city of ....
(a) Argentina (b) Sudan
(c) South Africa (d) Brazil

12. .... is the capital city of Greece.
(a) Thimphu (b) Paris
(c) Ottawa (d) Athens

13. Which of the following is the capital city of Australia?
(a) Sydney (b) New South Wales
(c) Canberra (d) Perth

14. Complete the given analogy.
South Korea : Seoul :: Maldives : ?
(a) Doha (b) Male
(c) Kuala Lumpur (d) Kathmandu

15. The capital of United States of America is ....
(a) New York (b) California
(c) Washington DC (d) Chicago

16. Complete the given analogy.
America : Dollar :: Bangladesh : ?
(a) Riyal (b) Taka
(c) Rupee (d) Renminbi

17. Identify the name of the currency as shown in the image given below.

(a) Chinese Renminbi (b) American Dollar
(c) Pakistani Rupee (d) Saudi Riyal

18. .... is the name of the currency of Japan.
(a) Taka (b) Rupee
(c) Dollar (d) Yen

19. Complete the given analogy.
Kuwait : Dinar :: Russia : ?
(a) Rubble (b) Yuan
(c) Pound (d) Euro

20. .... is the name of the currency of England.
(a) Pound (b) Peso
(c) Euro (d) Dollar

21. Which of the following countries is also known as 'The Gift of Nile'?
(a) Egypt (b) Cambodia
(c) Burkina Faso (d) Djibouti

22. Which of the following countries is the only nation that does not have a rectangular flag?
(a) China (b) Bhutan
(c) Nepal (d) Bangladesh

23. Tata Iron and Steel Company (TISCO) Limited was established in year............... in ....
(a) 1907, Jamshedpur
(b) 1906, Bhilai
(c) 1908, Bokaro
(d) 1909, Surat

MCQs 2 Marks Questions

24. Match the following.

List I (Country)	**List II** (Capital)
A. Austria	1. Cairo
B. Iraq	2. Dhaka
C. Egypt	3. Vienna
D. Bangladesh	4. Baghdad

Codes

	A	B	C	D		A	B	C	D
(a)	3	4	1	2	(b)	1	2	4	3
(c)	2	4	3	1	(d)	4	2	1	3

25. Match the following.

List I (International Organisation)	**List II** (Headquarter)
A. UNO	1. Geneva
B. IMF	2. Washington DC
C. WTO	3. New York
D. UNESCO	4. Paris

Codes

	A	B	C	D		A	B	C	D
(a)	3	2	1	4	(b)	1	3	4	2
(c)	2	1	3	4	(d)	4	2	1	3

26. Read the following statements and choose the correct option.

I. Kalidasa wrote the book 'Meghaduta'.

II. The epic 'Ramayana' was written by Valmiki.

Codes

(a) Only I (b) Only II

(c) Both I and II (d) None of these

27. Read the following statements and choose the correct option.

I. The full form of ILO is Indian Labour Organisation.

II. FAO has its headquarters at Rome, Italy.

Codes

(a) Only I (b) Only II

(c) Both I and II (d) None of these

28. Read the given statements and select the option that correctly identifies true (T) and false (F) ones.

I. Asian Development Bank has its headquarter at Manila, Philippines.

II. The Hemis National Park is located in Jammu and Kashmir.

III. The book Kadambari was written by Banabhatta.

IV. The United Nations General Assembly is also called the World's Parliament.

Codes

	I	II	III	IV		I	II	III	IV
(a)	T	T	F	F	(b)	T	T	F	T
(c)	T	T	T	T	(d)	F	F	F	T

29. There are two statements marked as Assertion (A) and Reason (R). Mark your answer as per the codes given below.

Assertion (A) Bangladesh is called the land of golden fiber.

Reason (R) Bangladesh is one of the largest jute producing countries in the world.

Codes

(a) Both A and R are true and R is the correct explanation of A

(b) Both A and R are true, but R is not the correct explanation of A

(c) A is true, but R is false

(d) A is false, but R is true

Darken your choice with HB Pencil

1. ⓐ ⓑ ⓒ ⓓ	6. ⓐ ⓑ ⓒ ⓓ	11. ⓐ ⓑ ⓒ ⓓ	16. ⓐ ⓑ ⓒ ⓓ	21. ⓐ ⓑ ⓒ ⓓ	26. ⓐ ⓑ ⓒ ⓓ
2. ⓐ ⓑ ⓒ ⓓ	7. ⓐ ⓑ ⓒ ⓓ	12. ⓐ ⓑ ⓒ ⓓ	17. ⓐ ⓑ ⓒ ⓓ	22. ⓐ ⓑ ⓒ ⓓ	27. ⓐ ⓑ ⓒ ⓓ
3. ⓐ ⓑ ⓒ ⓓ	8. ⓐ ⓑ ⓒ ⓓ	13. ⓐ ⓑ ⓒ ⓓ	18. ⓐ ⓑ ⓒ ⓓ	23. ⓐ ⓑ ⓒ ⓓ	28. ⓐ ⓑ ⓒ ⓓ
4. ⓐ ⓑ ⓒ ⓓ	9. ⓐ ⓑ ⓒ ⓓ	14. ⓐ ⓑ ⓒ ⓓ	19. ⓐ ⓑ ⓒ ⓓ	24. ⓐ ⓑ ⓒ ⓓ	29. ⓐ ⓑ ⓒ ⓓ
5. ⓐ ⓑ ⓒ ⓓ	10. ⓐ ⓑ ⓒ ⓓ	15. ⓐ ⓑ ⓒ ⓓ	20. ⓐ ⓑ ⓒ ⓓ	25. ⓐ ⓑ ⓒ ⓓ	

Practice Set 01

Time : 60 Mins. Max. Marks : 60

General Instructions

1. This question paper contains 50 questions.
2. All questions are compulsory. There is no negative marking.
3. Q. No. 1 to 40 are of 1 mark each and Q. No. 41 to 50 are of 2 marks each.
4. Use HB pencil / Blue ball point pen to mark your choice of answer by darkening the circles on the OMR Sheet.

MCQs 1 Mark Questions

1. Which among the following continents is the coldest, windiest and driest in the Earth ?
(a) Antarctica
(b) Africa
(c) Asia
(d) Australia

2. Identify which among the following does not belong to India's major large scale industries.
(a) Cotton textile industry
(b) Iron and steel industry
(c) Jute industry
(d) Khadi and village industry

3. Which one of the following is the longest National Highway in India ?
(a) National Highway 5
(b) National Highway 2
(c) National Highway 44
(d) National Highway 12

4. .... is also known as the Lower Chamber.
(a) Lok Sabha (b) Rajya Sabha
(c) Parliament (d) None of these

5. Which of the following celestial bodies bears 'the Sea of Tranquility' and 'the Ocean of Storms' ?
(a) Venus
(b) Moon
(c) Sun
(d) Earth

6. Which of the following National Highways connects the four metro cities of India (Delhi, Mumbai, Kolkata and Chennai)?
(a) National Highway-44
(b) National Highway-47A
(c) Golden Quadrilateral (GQ)
(d) North-South Corridor of NHDP

7. Which of the following is not an element of weather and climate ?
(a) Atmospheric pressure
(b) Temperature
(c) Altitude
(d) Humidity

8. Identify the name of person who first enter in space.
(a) Alan Shepard
(b) Valentina Tereshkova
(c) Yuri Gagarin
(d) Edward H White

9. The Atacama Desert, the world driest place on the Earth is situated in which of the following continents?
(a) Asia (b) Africa
(c) Australia (d) South America

10. Who among the following is the author of Vande Mataram ?
(a) Rabindranath Tagore
(b) Mahatma Gandhi
(c) Bankim Chandra Chatterjee
(d) Raja Ram Mohan Roy

11. Under which of the following articles of the Indian Constitution, individual go to the Supreme Court for the enforcement of a Fundamental Right?
(a) Article 33 (b) Article 32
(c) Article 37 (d) Article 40

12. Which of the following sectors is/are characterised by small and scattered units largely outside the control of the government ?
(a) Organised sector
(b) Unorganised sector
(c) Both (a) and (b)
(d) Neither (a) nor (b)

13. Identify the painting as depicted in the picture given below.

(a) Miniature painting
(b) Madhubani painting
(c) Kalamkari painting
(d) Warli painting

14. Which of the following states is/are connected to the HVJ pipeline ?
(a) Gujarat
(b) Rajasthan
(c) Madhya Pradesh
(d) All of the above

15. National emergency belongs to which article of the Indian Constitution?
(a) Article 376 (b) Article 352
(c) Article 360 (d) Article 355

16. ....is an asset that the borrower owns and uses this as a guarantee to a lender until the loan is repaid.
(a) Debt (b) Collateral
(c) Credit Card (d) Deposits

17. Identify the famous personality who was Educationist, author and scholar of Arabic and he was the first Education minister of India.
(a) Abul Kalam Azad
(b) Asaf Ali
(c) Jaipal Singh
(d) TT Krishnamachari

18. Financial Emergency belongs to which article of the Indian Constitution?
(a) Article 360 (b) Article 356
(c) Article 352 (d) Article 355

19. Name the light combat aircraft developed by India indigenously.
(a) Brahmos (b) Tejas
(c) Chetak (d) Astra

20. Which among the following places of India experiences the highest summer temperatures ?
(a) Pahalgam
(b) Leh
(c) Thiruvananthapuram
(d) Jaisalmer

21. .... is the head of the government in India.
(a) President (b) Prime Minister
(c) Governor (d) Speaker

22. Who was the first female to get Norman Borlaug award ?
(a) PT Usha
(b) Dr Amrita Patel
(c) Devika Rani
(d) Amrita Pritam

23. Identify the incorrectly matched pair.

	Nations		**Capitals**
(a)	Chile	–	Santiago
(b)	Argentina	–	Buenos Aires
(c)	North Korea	–	Seoul
(d)	Ethiopia	–	Addis Ababa

24. Which of the following leaders has authored the book 'Indian Struggle' ?
(a) Mahatma Gandhi
(b) Subhash Chandra Bose
(c) Jawaharlal Nehru
(d) Bipin Chandra Pal

25. Which of the following is associated with the iron found in the upper Ganga Valley for the first time ?
(a) Black and red ware
(b) Painted grey ware
(c) Black and grey ware
(d) Northern black polished ware

26. Identify the ruler who built 'Alai Darwaza'.
(a) Akbar
(b) Jahangir
(c) Alauddin Khilji
(d) Muhammad bin Tughluq

27. Which of the following groups supported the weimer republic ?
(a) Socialists (b) Catholics
(c) Democrats (d) All of these

28. Which among the following parts of Himalayas located between Teesta and Brahmaputra rivers ?
(a) Assam Himalayas
(b) Nepal Himalayas
(c) Kumaon Himalayas
(d) Himachal Himalayas

29. Suez Canal is located in which of the following countries ?
(a) Sudan (b) Saudi Arabia
(c) Egypt (d) Jordan

30. Identify the type of vegetation which is found in the higher reaches of the Himalayas.
(a) Tropical
(b) Alpine
(c) Temperature
(d) Sub-tropical

31. Which national waterway connect Allahabad to Haldia via Patna?
(a) National Waterway-2
(b) National Waterway-1
(c) National Waterway-3
(d) National Waterway-4

32. Which of the following crops is generally sown to restore and maintain soil fertility ?
(a) Barley (b) Jowar
(c) Maize (d) Pulses

33. In which year, TISCO the first major steel producing company established in India at Jamshedpur ?
(a) 1906 (b) 1908
(c) 1907 (d) 1910

34. Identify amongst the following is a static that measures the number of death per 1000 people.
(a) Infant Mortality Rate
(b) Maternal Mortality Rate
(c) Crude Death Rate
(d) Total Fertility Rate

35. Which body acts as the guardian of Fundamental Rights ?
(a) Supreme Court
(b) District Court
(c) Election Commission
(d) Legislature

36. Who among the following is the presiding officer of the Lok Sabha ?
(a) Vice-President
(b) Speaker
(c) President
(d) Prime Minister

37. Which of the following is not a Panchayati Raj Institution ?
(a) Gram Sabha
(b) Gram Co-operative Society
(c) Gram Panchayat
(d) Nyaya Panchayat

38. Which of these is permitted under the code of conduct for election campaigns ?
(a) Use of place of worship for election propaganda
(b) Use of government vehicles for election
(c) Use of media
(d) Once election are announced, making any promises of providing public facilities.

39. The term 'Googly' is associated with which of the following sports ?
(a) Hockey
(b) Badminton
(c) Cricket
(d) Football

40. What refers to the number of people in different age groups in a country?
(a) The age composition of a population
(b) Migration
(c) Population growth
(d) None of the above

MCQs 2 Marks Questions

41. Match the following.

List I (Components)	List II (Related to)
A. Biosphere	1. Blanket of air which surrounds the Earth
B. Atmosphere	2. Narrow zone where land, water and air interact
C. Hydrosphere	3. Domain of water
D. Environment	4. Our surroundings

Codes

	A	B	C	D		A	B	C	D
(a)	2	1	3	4	(b)	1	3	2	4
(c)	3	1	4	2	(d)	3	1	2	4

42. There are two statements marked as Assertion (A) and Reason (R). Mark your answer as per the codes given below.

Assertion (A) The Indian Constitution came into force with effect from 26th January, 1950.

Reason (R) At the time of its adoption, the Constitution of India contained 395 Articles and 8 Schedules.

Codes
(a) Both A and R are true and R is the correct explanation of A
(b) Both A and R are true, but R is not the correct explanation of A
(c) A is true, but R is false
(d) A is false, but R is true

43. Identify the event with the help of the information given below.
- It was the first Non-Cooperation Movement by Mahatma Gandhi. Due to failure of crops, the farmers with Gandhiji with held the revenue to get remission based on revenue code.

(a) Champaran Satyagraha
(b) Kheda Satyagraha
(c) Ahmedabad Satyagraha
(d) Rowlatt Satyagraha

44. Which of the following factors affecting location of industries ?

I. Availability of raw materials
II. Government subsidies
III. Availability of labour
IV. Capital Availability

Select the correct option.

(a) I and II
(b) II and III
(c) I, II and III
(d) All of the above

45. Read the given statements and select the option that correctly identifies true (T) and false (F) ones.

I. The Right to Equality ensures equality before the law.
II. The NHRC is an independent commission set up in 1993.
III. The summon is an order issued by a court asking a person to appear before it.
IV. A secular state is one that establish any one religion as official religion.

Codes

	I	II	III	IV
(a)	T	T	T	F
(b)	F	T	F	F
(c)	T	T	F	T
(d)	F	F	T	T

46. There are two statements marked as Assertion (A) and Reason (R). Mark your answer as per the codes given below.

Assertion (A) Chandragupta overthrew the Nanda Dynasty and then campaigned in Central and Northern India.

Reason (R) He is credited with bringing together the small fragmented kingdoms of the country and combining them into a single large empire.

Codes

(a) Both A and R are true and R is the correct explanation of A
(b) Both A and R are true, but R is not the correct explanation of A
(c) A is true, but R is false
(d) A is false, but R is true

47. There are two statements marked as Assertion (A) and Reason (R). Mark your answer as per the codes given below.

Assertion (A) The currency notes and coin are called legal tenders.

Reason (R) They can't be refused by any citizen of the country for settlement of any kind of transaction.

Codes

(a) Both A and R are true and R is the correct explanation of A
(b) Both A and R are true, but R is not the correct explanation of A
(c) A is true, but R is false
(d) A is false, but R is true

48. Which of the following are the features of the Directive Principles of State Policy?

I. They are non-justiciable.
II. They are enumerated in Part IV of the Constitution.
III. They are positive in nature.
IV. They shall be enforceable by courts.

Codes

(a) I, II and III
(b) II, III and IV
(c) I, II and IV
(d) I, III and IV

49. Read the given statements and select the option that correctly identifies true (T) and false (F) ones.

I. The centripital force is an apparant force caused by the Earth's rotation.

II. The Thar desert experiences the highest range of temperature in a day.

III. The maritime climate is experienced in coastal areas.

IV. The climate of India may be described as temperature monsoon.

Codes

	I	II	III	IV		I	II	III	IV
(a)	T	T	T	F	(b)	T	F	T	F
(c)	F	T	F	T	(d)	F	F	T	T

50. Consider the following statements and select the correct option.

I. Louis XVI was sentenced to death by a court in the charge of Treason.

II. The period from 1793 to 1794 is referred to as the Region of Prosperity.

Codes

(a) Only I (b) Only II

(c) Both I and II (d) Neither I nor II

Darken your choice with HB Pencil

1. (a) (b) (c) (d)	10. (a) (b) (c) (d)	19. (a) (b) (c) (d)	28. (a) (b) (c) (d)	37. (a) (b) (c) (d)	46. (a) (b) (c) (d)
2. (a) (b) (c) (d)	11. (a) (b) (c) (d)	20. (a) (b) (c) (d)	29. (a) (b) (c) (d)	38. (a) (b) (c) (d)	47. (a) (b) (c) (d)
3. (a) (b) (c) (d)	12. (a) (b) (c) (d)	21. (a) (b) (c) (d)	30. (a) (b) (c) (d)	39. (a) (b) (c) (d)	48. (a) (b) (c) (d)
4. (a) (b) (c) (d)	13. (a) (b) (c) (d)	22. (a) (b) (c) (d)	31. (a) (b) (c) (d)	40. (a) (b) (c) (d)	49. (a) (b) (c) (d)
5. (a) (b) (c) (d)	14. (a) (b) (c) (d)	23. (a) (b) (c) (d)	32. (a) (b) (c) (d)	41. (a) (b) (c) (d)	50. (a) (b) (c) (d)
6. (a) (b) (c) (d)	15. (a) (b) (c) (d)	24. (a) (b) (c) (d)	33. (a) (b) (c) (d)	42. (a) (b) (c) (d)	
7. (a) (b) (c) (d)	16. (a) (b) (c) (d)	25. (a) (b) (c) (d)	34. (a) (b) (c) (d)	43. (a) (b) (c) (d)	
8. (a) (b) (c) (d)	17. (a) (b) (c) (d)	26. (a) (b) (c) (d)	35. (a) (b) (c) (d)	44. (a) (b) (c) (d)	
9. (a) (b) (c) (d)	18. (a) (b) (c) (d)	27. (a) (b) (c) (d)	36. (a) (b) (c) (d)	45. (a) (b) (c) (d)	

Practice Set 02

Time : 60 Mins. Max. Marks : 60

General Instructions

1. This question paper contains 50 questions.
2. All questions are compulsory. There is no negative marking.
3. Q. No. 1 to 40 are of 1 mark each and Q. No. 41 to 50 are of 2 marks each.
4. Use HB pencil / Blue ball point pen to mark your choice of answer by darkening the circles on the OMR Sheet.

MCQs 1 Mark Questions

1. Which of the following is/are the source(s) of funds for the Panchayat?
(a) Tax collection
(b) Donation
(c) Both (a) and (b)
(d) Loans from nationalised banks

2. Who among the following is regarded as the 'Father of Modern India'?
(a) Sir Aurobindo
(b) Swami Dayananda Saraswati
(c) Raja Ram Mohan Roy
(d) Mahatma Gandhi

3. Who was the first woman to became a Chief Election Commissioner of India?
(a) VS Ramadevi (b) GD Das
(c) SK Bedi (d) RM Nikam

4. Choose the incorrectly matched pair.

	State	Festival
(a)	Arunachal Pradesh	– Losar
(b)	Andhra Pradesh	– Ugadi
(c)	Kerala	– Onam
(d)	Assam	– Kharchi

5. Identify the name of the scientist who proved that the path of each planet around the Sun is elliptical.
(a) Kepler (b) Galileo
(c) Newton (d) Copernicus

6. Which of the following constellations help to locate the pole star ?
(a) Orion (b) Ursa Major
(c) Virgo (d) Leo

7. Which among the following is a component of upper air circulation ?
(a) North-Easterlies
(b) Jet Stream
(c) South-West monsoon
(d) Kal Baisakhi

8. Which of the following gives the correct information regarding the solar eclipse?
(a) Sun is between the Moon and the Earth
(b) Earth is between the Sun and the Moon
(c) Moon is between the Earth and the Sun
(d) None of the above

9. The Marina Beach, the world's second longest beach is situated in which of the following continents?
(a) Asia
(b) Africa
(c) North America
(d) Europe

10. The 'lake Assal', the world lowest point on land situated in which continent ?
(a) Africa
(b) Europe
(c) Asia
(d) North America

11. What does the 5 rings of Olympic signify?
(a) Countries
(b) Continents
(c) Oceans
(d) 5 elements of nature

12. Which of the following is/are included in the secondary sector ?
(a) Manufacturing
(b) Construction
(c) Both (a) and (b)
(d) Health

13. Which National Highway connects Delhi and Amritsar?
(a) NH-1 (b) NH-2
(c) NH-7 (d) NH-10

14. Which among the following ports is/are located on the Western coast of India ?
(a) Cochin (b) Haldia
(c) Ennore (d) Both (b) and (c)

15. Identify the name of the award as shown in the image given below.

(a) Bharat Ratna
(b) Dronacharya Award
(c) Arjuna Award
(d) Rajiv Gandhi Khel Ratna Award

16. The banks charge a higher interest rate on loans than what they offer on ……
(a) withdrawls
(b) deposits
(c) loans
(d) demand drafts

17. The term ……… and ……… were added in Preamble through the 42nd Constitutional Amendment Act, 1976.
(a) socialist, liberty (b) justice, secular
(c) socialist, secular(d) equality, fraternity

18. Which article of the Indian Constitution, the procedure of Amendment of Constitution is mentioned?
(a) Article 366 (b) Article 368
(c) Article 367 (d) Article 369

19. What does PSLV stand for ?
(a) Polar Satellite Launch Vehicle
(b) Polished Satellite Launch Vehicle
(c) Preparatory Satellite Launch Vehicle
(d) Polar Surface Launch Vehicle

20. Which one of the following refers to the first nuclear reactor of India ?
(a) Kamini
(b) Apsara
(c) Urvashi
(d) Rohini

21. Identify the name of first scientist of Indian origin, who got Nobel Prize in the field of medical science.
(a) CV Raman
(b) Har Gobind Khorana
(c) Subrahmanyam Chandrasekhar
(d) Amartya Sen

22. The Shanti Swarup Bhatnagar award is given for which among the following fields?
(a) Film (b) Music
(c) Science (d) Journalism

23. Identify the famous person who was considered as the 'Father of Indian Space Program'.
(a) Homi J Bhabha
(b) Dr Vikram Sarabhai
(c) Satish Dhawan
(d) Satyendranath Bose

24. Name the personality who wrote the famous book 'Gita Govinda'.
(a) Chanakya (b) Shudraka
(c) Jayadeva (d) Patanjali

25. Who among the following was the first Jain Tirthankara ?
(a) Ajitanatha (b) Rishabhanatha
(c) Parshvanatha (d) Mahavira

26. Identify the famous monument of India as show in the picture given below.

(a) Humayun Tomb
(b) Safdarjung's Tomb
(c) Tomb of Iltutmish
(d) Tomb of Sher Shah Suri

27. Identify the events which is/are important in the making of the modern world.
(a) French Revolution
(b) Russian Revolution
(c) Rize of Nazism
(d) Both (a) and (c)

28. Which of the following is the highest peak in the Eastern Ghats ?
(a) Anamudi (b) Mahendragiri
(c) Guru Shikhar (d) Nanda Devi

29. Identify the place which is known as the 'coffee port' of the world.
(a) Sao Paulo (b) Santos
(c) Rio de Janeiro (d) Buenos Aires

30. Choose the incorrectly matched pair.

	National Park		State
(a)	Rajaji National Park	–	Uttarakhand
(b)	Dudhwa National Park	–	Uttar Pradesh
(c)	Kaziranga National Park	–	Arunachal Pradesh
(d)	Keoladeo Ghana National Park	–	Rajasthan

31. Which of the following has coined the term 'Ecosystem' for the first time ?
(a) Lindeman (b) Odum
(c) AG Tansley (d) Haeckel

32. Which of the following is not a cash crop ?
(a) Cotton
(b) Groundnut
(c) Jowar
(d) Jute

33. Identify the name of industry which is known as 'backbone of the modern industries'.
(a) Iron and Steel Industry
(b) Cotton Textile Industry
(c) Information Technology
(d) Animation Industry

34. What is the study of human populations, their size, composition and distribution across space is called ?
(a) Census
(b) Demography
(c) Population change
(d) Natural growth rate

35. What does the term 'PIL' stand for ?
(a) People's Interest Litigation
(b) Public Interest Law
(c) Public International Litigation
(d) Public Interest Litigation

36. Who has the the power to summon and prologue either house of Parliament or to dissolve Lok Sabha ?
(a) Prime Minister
(b) President
(c) Speaker of Lok Sabha
(d) Judge of Supreme Court

37. The .... is also known as the 'Powerhouse of the Cell'.
(a) cell membrane (b) nucleus
(c) cytoplasm (d) mitochondria

38. What is the minimum age required to contest on election to Rajya Sabha ?
(a) 18 years (b) 30 years
(c) 25 years (d) 35 years

39. Identify the incorrectly matched pair.

	Nations		National Games
(a)	USA	–	Baseball
(b)	Pakistan	–	Field Hockey
(c)	China	–	Table tennis
(d)	India	–	Cricket

40. Who wrote the famous book 'Arthashastra'?
(a) Kautilya (b) Ved Vyas
(c) Ashwaghosh (d) Jayadev

MCQs 2 Marks Questions

41. Which of the following are the challenges faced by Panchayati Raj in India?
I. Lack of finances
II. Administrative problem
III. Political interference
IV. Over population
Codes
(a) I, II and III (b) II and IV
(c) II and III (d) All of these

42. There are two statements marked as Assertion (A) and Reason (R). Mark your answer as per the codes given below.
Assertion (A) The 73rd Constitutional Amendment Act grant constitutional status to the Gram Sabha.
Reason (R) The Balwant Rai Mehta Committee mentioned in the Gram Sabha.
Codes
(a) Both A and R are true and R is the correct explanation of A
(b) Both A and R are true, but R is not the correct explanation of A
(c) A is true, but R is false
(d) A is false, but R is true

43. Identify the event with the help of the information given below.
- It was held in London on 12th November 1930, to discuss Simon Commission Report.
- It was the conference arranged between the British and Indians as equal.

(a) First Round Table Conference
(b) Gandhi Irvin Pact
(c) Poona Pact
(d) Third Round Table Conference

44. Which of the following countries fought in Second World War?
I. Italy
II. France
III. USSR
IV. Japan
Choose the correct option.
(a) I and II
(b) I,II and III
(c) I,III and IV
(d) All of the above

45. Identify the name of ocean with the help of the information given below.

- It is the largest and deepest ocean. The most of the islands of the ocean are volcanic or coral origin. The Mariana Trench, the world's deepest trench is located in this ocean.

(a) Atlantic Ocean
(b) Pacific Ocean
(c) Indian Ocean
(d) Arctic Ocean

46. Match the following.

List I	List II
A. Human Trafficking	1. Buying and selling of men and women for immoral purpose
B. Rights	2. A person belonging to a low caste
C. Dalit	3. Claims of persons recognised by society and sanctioned by law

Codes

	A	B	C
(a)	1	2	3
(b)	2	1	3
(c)	2	3	1
(d)	1	3	2

47. There are two statements marked as Assertion (A) and Reason (R). Mark your answer as per the codes given below.

Assertion (A) India is the largest producer of raw jute and jute goods.

Reason (R) The small and marginal farmers are engaged in the production of jute.

Codes

(a) Both A and R are true and R is the correct explanation of A
(b) Both A and R are true, but R is not the correct explanation of A
(c) A is true, but R is false
(d) A is false, but R is true

48. Identify the correctly matched pair(s).

National Highway		Cities Connected
I. NH–4	–	Chennai and Hyderabad
II. NH–8	–	Delhi to Mumbai
III. NH–5	–	Ahmedabad and Jodhpur

Codes

(a) Both I and II (b) Only II
(c) II and III (d) All of these

49. Match the following.

List I (Man-made Disaster)	List II (Year)
A. Three Miles Tragedy	1. 2011
B. Bhopal Gas Tragedy	2. 1986
C. Chernobyl Nuclear Disaster	3. 1984
D. Fukushima Nuclear Disaster	4. 1979

Codes

	A	B	C	D
(a)	3	4	2	1
(b)	4	3	2	1
(c)	3	4	1	2
(d)	4	3	1	2

50. Identify the national park located in Indian state as marked on the map given below.

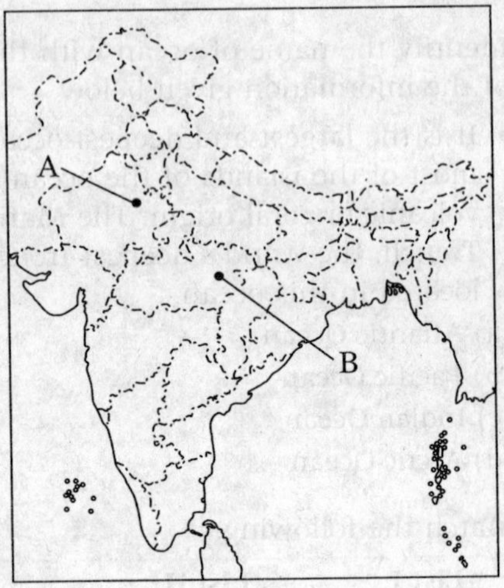

	A	B
(a)	Gir	Jim Corbett
(b)	Sariska	Gir
(c)	Sariska	Kanha
(d)	Kanha	Jim Corbett

Darken your choice with HB Pencil

1. ⓐ ⓑ ⓒ ⓓ	10. ⓐ ⓑ ⓒ ⓓ	19. ⓐ ⓑ ⓒ ⓓ	28. ⓐ ⓑ ⓒ ⓓ	37. ⓐ ⓑ ⓒ ⓓ	46. ⓐ ⓑ ⓒ ⓓ
2. ⓐ ⓑ ⓒ ⓓ	11. ⓐ ⓑ ⓒ ⓓ	20. ⓐ ⓑ ⓒ ⓓ	29. ⓐ ⓑ ⓒ ⓓ	38. ⓐ ⓑ ⓒ ⓓ	47. ⓐ ⓑ ⓒ ⓓ
3. ⓐ ⓑ ⓒ ⓓ	12. ⓐ ⓑ ⓒ ⓓ	21. ⓐ ⓑ ⓒ ⓓ	30. ⓐ ⓑ ⓒ ⓓ	39. ⓐ ⓑ ⓒ ⓓ	48. ⓐ ⓑ ⓒ ⓓ
4. ⓐ ⓑ ⓒ ⓓ	13. ⓐ ⓑ ⓒ ⓓ	22. ⓐ ⓑ ⓒ ⓓ	31. ⓐ ⓑ ⓒ ⓓ	40. ⓐ ⓑ ⓒ ⓓ	49. ⓐ ⓑ ⓒ ⓓ
5. ⓐ ⓑ ⓒ ⓓ	14. ⓐ ⓑ ⓒ ⓓ	23. ⓐ ⓑ ⓒ ⓓ	32. ⓐ ⓑ ⓒ ⓓ	41. ⓐ ⓑ ⓒ ⓓ	50. ⓐ ⓑ ⓒ ⓓ
6. ⓐ ⓑ ⓒ ⓓ	15. ⓐ ⓑ ⓒ ⓓ	24. ⓐ ⓑ ⓒ ⓓ	33. ⓐ ⓑ ⓒ ⓓ	42. ⓐ ⓑ ⓒ ⓓ	
7. ⓐ ⓑ ⓒ ⓓ	16. ⓐ ⓑ ⓒ ⓓ	25. ⓐ ⓑ ⓒ ⓓ	34. ⓐ ⓑ ⓒ ⓓ	43. ⓐ ⓑ ⓒ ⓓ	
8. ⓐ ⓑ ⓒ ⓓ	17. ⓐ ⓑ ⓒ ⓓ	26. ⓐ ⓑ ⓒ ⓓ	35. ⓐ ⓑ ⓒ ⓓ	44. ⓐ ⓑ ⓒ ⓓ	
9. ⓐ ⓑ ⓒ ⓓ	18. ⓐ ⓑ ⓒ ⓓ	27. ⓐ ⓑ ⓒ ⓓ	36. ⓐ ⓑ ⓒ ⓓ	45. ⓐ ⓑ ⓒ ⓓ	

Answer Sheet

Chapter 01

1. (c)	**2.** (b)	**3.** (b)	**4.** (a)	**5.** (b)	**6.** (b)	**7.** (a)	**8.** (b)	**9.** (c)	**10.** (d)
11. (b)	**12.** (a)	**13.** (c)	**14.** (b)	**15.** (c)	**16.** (c)	**17.** (b)	**18.** (a)	**19.** (b)	**20.** (a)
21. (a)	**22.** (c)	**23.** (a)	**24.** (a)	**25.** (a)	**26.** (d)	**27.** (d)	**28.** (a)	**29.** (d)	**30.** (c)
31. (c)	**32.** (a)	**33.** (c)							

Chapter 02

1. (c)	**2.** (c)	**3.** (b)	**4.** (d)	**5.** (c)	**6.** (c)	**7.** (a)	**8.** (b)	**9.** (b)	**10.** (c)
11. (c)	**12.** (c)	**13.** (c)	**14.** (a)	**15.** (a)	**16.** (d)	**17.** (c)	**18.** (a)	**19.** (a)	**20.** (b)
21. (c)	**22.** (b)	**23.** (c)	**24.** (c)	**25.** (d)	**26.** (c)	**27.** (a)	**28.** (b)		

Chapter 03

1. (c)	**2.** (d)	**3.** (b)	**4.** (c)	**5.** (c)	**6.** (d)	**7.** (b)	**8.** (a)	**9.** (a)	**10.** (a)
11. (a)	**12.** (a)	**13.** (b)	**14.** (d)	**15.** (a)	**16.** (a)	**17.** (b)	**18.** (a)	**19.** (b)	**20.** (a)
21. (a)	**22.** (c)	**23.** (b)	**24.** (b)						

Chapter 04

1. (a)	**2.** (d)	**3.** (b)	**4.** (a)	**5.** (a)	**6.** (a)	**7.** (b)	**8.** (b)	**9.** (d)	**10.** (b)
11. (c)	**12.** (d)	**13.** (c)	**14.** (c)	**15.** (a)	**16.** (c)	**17.** (d)	**18.** (a)	**19.** (b)	**20.** (a)
21. (d)	**22.** (d)	**23.** (b)	**24.** (a)	**25.** (a)	**26.** (b)	**27.** (a)			

Chapter 05

1. (c)	**2.** (c)	**3.** (d)	**4.** (c)	**5.** (b)	**6.** (b)	**7.** (b)	**8.** (d)	**9.** (d)	**10.** (c)
11. (d)	**12.** (c)	**13.** (d)	**14.** (b)	**15.** (a)	**16.** (b)	**17.** (a)	**18.** (d)	**19.** (d)	**20.** (d)
21. (b)	**22.** (c)	**23.** (a)	**24.** (a)	**25.** (d)	**26.** (b)				

Chapter 06

1. (b)	**2.** (c)	**3.** (c)	**4.** (a)	**5.** (d)	**6.** (a)	**7.** (c)	**8.** (a)	**9.** (a)	**10.** (b)
11. (d)	**12.** (a)	**13.** (c)	**14.** (b)	**15.** (c)	**16.** (c)	**17.** (d)	**18.** (a)	**19.** (a)	**20.** (c)
21. (a)	**22.** (d)	**23.** (a)	**24.** (b)	**25.** (b)	**26.** (c)	**27.** (a)	**28.** (d)	**29.** (a)	**30.** (c)
31. (a)	**32.** (b)								

Chapter 07

1. (c)	**2.** (d)	**3.** (b)	**4.** (a)	**5.** (c)	**6.** (c)	**7.** (d)	**8.** (a)	**9.** (a)	**10.** (a)
11. (b)	**12.** (a)	**13.** (d)	**14.** (c)	**15.** (b)	**16.** (c)	**17.** (c)	**18.** (b)	**19.** (c)	**20.** (b)
21. (d)	**22.** (d)	**23.** (b)	**24.** (a)	**25.** (b)	**26.** (b)	**27.** (a)	**28.** (c)	**29.** (d)	**30.** (d)
31. (d)	**32.** (b)	**33.** (a)	**34.** (a)	**35.** (a)					

Chapter 08

1. (b)	**2.** (b)	**3.** (c)	**4.** (a)	**5.** (b)	**6.** (b)	**7.** (d)	**8.** (a)	**9.** (b)	**10.** (d)
11. (c)	**12.** (d)	**13.** (b)	**14.** (d)	**15.** (a)	**16.** (b)	**17.** (b)	**18.** (d)	**19.** (b)	**20.** (c)
21. (c)	**22.** (c)	**23.** (d)	**24.** (b)	**25.** (c)	**26.** (a)	**27.** (b)	**28.** (b)	**29.** (c)	**30.** (b)

Chapter 09

1. (d)	**2.** (d)	**3.** (c)	**4.** (c)	**5.** (d)	**6.** (a)	**7.** (b)	**8.** (b)	**9.** (a)	**10.** (c)
11. (a)	**12.** (d)	**13.** (b)	**14.** (c)	**15.** (a)	**16.** (a)	**17.** (a)	**18.** (a)	**19.** (c)	**20.** (a)
21. (c)	**22.** (d)	**23.** (b)	**24.** (b)	**25.** (d)					

Chapter 10

1. (d)	**2.** (c)	**3.** (b)	**4.** (d)	**5.** (a)	**6.** (a)	**7.** (b)	**8.** (d)	**9.** (a)	**10.** (a)
11. (b)	**12.** (b)	**13.** (b)	**14.** (b)	**15.** (d)	**16.** (a)	**17.** (a)	**18.** (b)	**19.** (d)	**20.** (d)
21. (a)	**22.** (c)	**23.** (a)	**24.** (a)	**25.** (b)	**26.** (a)				

Chapter 11

1. (c)	**2.** (c)	**3.** (c)	**4.** (b)	**5.** (c)	**6.** (d)	**7.** (a)	**8.** (c)	**9.** (a)	**10.** (a)
11. (c)	**12.** (a)	**13.** (d)	**14.** (a)	**15.** (d)	**16.** (d)	**17.** (a)	**18.** (b)	**19.** (b)	**20.** (c)
21. (b)	**22.** (c)	**23.** (d)	**24.** (b)	**25.** (c)	**26.** (d)	**27.** (a)	**28.** (b)	**29.** (b)	**30.** (a)
31. (a)									

Chapter 12

1. (d)	**2.** (c)	**3.** (a)	**4.** (a)	**5.** (d)	**6.** (b)	**7.** (b)	**8.** (a)	**9.** (b)	**10.** (c)
11. (d)	**12.** (b)	**13.** (c)	**14.** (b)	**15.** (a)	**16.** (c)	**17.** (c)	**18.** (d)	**19.** (b)	**20.** (a)
21. (b)	**22.** (a)	**23.** (b)	**24.** (a)	**25.** (a)	**26.** (a)	**27.** (c)	**28.** (b)		

Chapter 13

1. (c)	**2.** (a)	**3.** (c)	**4.** (a)	**5.** (b)	**6.** (b)	**7.** (b)	**8.** (d)	**9.** (c)	**10.** (b)
11. (d)	**12.** (b)	**13.** (c)	**14.** (a)	**15.** (c)	**16.** (d)	**17.** (c)	**18.** (b)	**19.** (c)	**20.** (d)
21. (a)	**22.** (c)	**23.** (b)	**24.** (a)	**25.** (c)	**26.** (a)	**27.** (a)			

Chapter 14

1. (d)	**2.** (c)	**3.** (b)	**4.** (b)	**5.** (a)	**6.** (c)	**7.** (c)	**8.** (b)	**9.** (d)	**10.** (a)
11. (a)	**12.** (c)	**13.** (c)	**14.** (c)	**15.** (d)	**16.** (d)	**17.** (d)	**18.** (d)	**19.** (c)	**20.** (a)
21. (b)	**22.** (b)	**23.** (b)	**24.** (b)	**25.** (c)	**26.** (a)	**27.** (b)	**28.** (a)	**29.** (b)	**30.** (a)
31. (b)	**32.** (b)	**33.** (b)	**34.** (a)	**35.** (b)					

Chapter 15

1. (a)	**2.** (b)	**3.** (a)	**4.** (d)	**5.** (a)	**6.** (a)	**7.** (b)	**8.** (a)	**9.** (a)	**10.** (b)
11. (c)	**12.** (b)	**13.** (c)	**14.** (a)	**15.** (c)	**16.** (c)	**17.** (a)	**18.** (a)	**19.** (c)	**20.** (b)
21. (b)	**22.** (d)	**23.** (b)	**24.** (a)	**25.** (c)					

Chapter 16

1. (d)	**2.** (c)	**3.** (c)	**4.** (d)	**5.** (c)	**6.** (d)	**7.** (b)	**8.** (b)	**9.** (b)	**10.** (a)
11. (c)	**12.** (b)	**13.** (d)	**14.** (c)	**15.** (c)	**16.** (b)	**17.** (d)	**18.** (a)	**19.** (c)	**20.** (a)
21. (b)	**22.** (a)	**23.** (a)							

Chapter 17

1. (d)	**2.** (b)	**3.** (c)	**4.** (b)	**5.** (b)	**6.** (d)	**7.** (c)	**8.** (b)	**9.** (c)	**10.** (b)
11. (b)	**12.** (b)	**13.** (a)	**14.** (c)	**15.** (d)	**16.** (a)	**17.** (c)	**18.** (b)	**19.** (a)	**20.** (c)
21. (c)	**22.** (c)	**23.** (a)	**24.** (d)	**25.** (a)	**26.** (d)				

Chapter 18

1. (d)	**2.** (a)	**3.** (c)	**4.** (b)	**5.** (d)	**6.** (c)	**7.** (c)	**8.** (b)	**9.** (a)	**10.** (a)
11. (d)	**12.** (a)	**13.** (a)	**14.** (c)	**15.** (a)	**16.** (c)	**17.** (c)	**18.** (c)	**19.** (c)	**20.** (b)
21. (d)	**22.** (c)	**23.** (a)	**24.** (c)						

Chapter 19

1. (c)	**2.** (a)	**3.** (a)	**4.** (c)	**5.** (d)	**6.** (b)	**7.** (b)	**8.** (b)	**9.** (a)	**10.** (d)
11. (c)	**12.** (b)	**13.** (b)	**14.** (c)	**15.** (c)	**16.** (d)	**17.** (a)	**18.** (a)	**19.** (c)	**20.** (b)
21. (b)	**22.** (b)	**23.** (c)	**24.** (a)	**25.** (a)	**26.** (c)	**27.** (c)			

Chapter 20

1. (c)	**2.** (c)	**3.** (c)	**4.** (a)	**5.** (c)	**6.** (b)	**7.** (d)	**8.** (a)	**9.** (c)	**10.** (c)
11. (a)	**12.** (a)	**13.** (c)	**14.** (b)	**15.** (d)	**16.** (c)	**17.** (b)	**18.** (b)	**19.** (d)	**20.** (a)
21. (c)	**22.** (a)	**23.** (b)	**24.** (d)	**25.** (c)	**26.** (a)				

Chapter 21

1. (a)	**2.** (c)	**3.** (c)	**4.** (a)	**5.** (a)	**6.** (b)	**7.** (a)	**8.** (b)	**9.** (a)	**10.** (a)
11. (b)	**12.** (c)	**13.** (d)	**14.** (b)	**15.** (a)	**16.** (d)	**17.** (a)	**18.** (c)	**19.** (d)	**20.** (c)
21. (a)	**22.** (a)	**23.** (c)	**24.** (c)	**25.** (b)	**26.** (b)	**27.** (c)			

Chapter 22

1. (a)	**2.** (b)	**3.** (b)	**4.** (c)	**5.** (a)	**6.** (a)	**7.** (d)	**8.** (b)	**9.** (a)	**10.** (b)
11. (b)	**12.** (a)	**13.** (a)	**14.** (a)	**15.** (b)	**16.** (c)	**17.** (a)	**18.** (b)		

Chapter 23

1. (c)	**2.** (c)	**3.** (d)	**4.** (a)	**5.** (a)	**6.** (c)	**7.** (a)	**8.** (c)	**9.** (c)	**10.** (d)
11. (c)	**12.** (b)	**13.** (c)	**14.** (d)	**15.** (d)	**16.** (a)	**17.** (c)	**18.** (c)	**19.** (a)	**20.** (c)
21. (b)	**22.** (c)	**23.** (d)	**24.** (a)	**25.** (c)	**26.** (c)				

Chapter 24

1. (c)	2. (d)	3. (b)	4. (d)	5. (a)	6. (a)	7. (a)	8. (a)	9. (a)	10. (c)
11. (a)	12. (b)	13. (b)	14. (a)	15. (b)	16. (c)	17. (d)	18. (c)	19. (b)	20. (b)
21. (b)	22. (c)	23. (a)	24. (d)	25. (b)	26. (d)	27. (d)	28. (a)	29. (c)	30. (a)

Chapter 25

1. (b)	2. (a)	3. (b)	4. (a)	5. (d)	6. (c)	7. (b)	8. (a)	9. (b)	10. (b)
11. (d)	12. (a)	13. (a)	14. (c)	15. (b)	16. (b)	17. (b)	18. (a)	19. (c)	20. (c)
21. (a)	22. (b)	23. (b)	24. (c)	25. (a)	26. (b)	27. (a)	28. (b)	29. (c)	

Chapter 26

1. (a)	2. (c)	3. (d)	4. (d)	5. (a)	6. (a)	7. (d)	8. (c)	9. (b)	10. (b)
11. (b)	12. (c)	13. (a)	14. (a)	15. (c)	16. (d)	17. (a)	18. (b)	19. (a)	20. (d)
21. (a)	22. (b)	23. (c)	24. (d)	25. (b)	26. (b)	27. (c)			

Chapter 27

1. (d)	2. (c)	3. (b)	4. (b)	5. (a)	6. (c)	7. (c)	8. (b)	9. (c)	10. (b)
11. (b)	12. (b)	13. (d)	14. (c)	15. (c)	16. (a)	17. (a)	18. (d)	19. (c)	20. (a)
21. (a)	22. (b)	23. (d)	24. (a)	25. (d)	26. (d)	27. (a)	28. (d)	29. (b)	

Chapter 28

1. (b)	2. (c)	3. (a)	4. (c)	5. (d)	6. (b)	7. (a)	8. (c)	9. (c)	10. (a)
11. (c)	12. (d)	13. (c)	14. (b)	15. (c)	16. (b)	17. (a)	18. (d)	19. (a)	20. (a)
21. (a)	22. (c)	23. (a)	24. (a)	25. (a)	26. (c)	27. (b)	28. (c)	29. (a)	

Practice Set 01

1. (a)	2. (d)	3. (c)	4. (a)	5. (b)	6. (c)	7. (c)	8. (c)	9. (d)	10. (c)
11. (b)	12. (b)	13. (d)	14. (d)	15. (b)	16. (b)	17. (a)	18. (a)	19. (b)	20. (d)
21. (b)	22. (b)	23. (c)	24. (b)	25. (b)	26. (c)	27. (d)	28. (a)	29. (c)	30. (b)
31. (b)	32. (d)	33. (c)	34. (c)	35. (a)	36. (b)	37. (b)	38. (d)	39. (c)	40. (a)
41. (a)	42. (b)	43. (b)	44. (d)	45. (a)	46. (b)	47. (a)	48. (a)	49. (a)	50. (a)

Practice Set 02

1. (c)	2. (c)	3. (a)	4. (d)	5. (a)	6. (b)	7. (b)	8. (c)	9. (a)	10. (a)
11. (b)	12. (c)	13. (a)	14. (a)	15. (c)	16. (b)	17. (c)	18. (b)	19. (a)	20. (b)
21. (b)	22. (c)	23. (b)	24. (c)	25. (b)	26. (a)	27. (d)	28. (b)	29. (b)	30. (c)
31. (c)	32. (c)	33. (a)	34. (b)	35. (d)	36. (b)	37. (d)	38. (b)	39. (d)	40. (a)
41. (a)	42. (b)	43. (a)	44. (d)	45. (b)	46. (d)	47. (b)	48. (b)	49. (b)	50. (c)